DANAE DOBSON

D0404450

Let's walk THE TALK!

girlfriend to girlfriend on faith,
friendship & finding real love

TYNDALE HOUSE PUBLISHERS, INC., CAROL STREAM, ILLINOIS

Visit Tyndale's exciting Web site at www.tyndale.com

TYNDALE and Tyndale's quill logo are registered trademarks of Tyndale House Publishers, Inc.

Let's Walk the Talk!: Girlfriend to Girlfriend on Faith, Friendship, and Finding Real Love

Cover design by Jennifer Ghionzoli and Ruth Berg

Interior design by Beth Sparkman

Library of Congress Cataloging-in-Publication Data

Dobson, Danae.
    Let's walk the talk! : girlfriend to girlfriend on faith, friendship, and finding real love / Danae Dobson.
       p. cm.
    ISBN 978-1-4143-0810-4 (sc)
    1. Girls—Religious life—Juvenile literature. I. Title.
    BV4551.3.D64 2009
    248.8'33—dc22   2009019564

Printed in the United States of America

15 14 13 12 11 10 09
 7   6   5   4   3   2   1

Contents

To Flo Waltrip, who has prayed for me daily since I was a teen. I will always be grateful to her for this expression of love and kindness.

Introduction

Do you ever wish you could get into the minds of other Christian teens and find out what they think about the issues you're concerned about? Would you like to ask them how they manage to survive and thrive while remaining true to their commitment to Christ? If so, then I have good news: I've already done the asking!

During the course of one year, I conducted table discussions, Internet chats, phone calls, and one-on-one conversations with people from various states and church backgrounds. I interviewed girls and guys, as well as youth leaders, teachers, and counselors on the matters that are important to you. Each person had something interesting and thought-provoking to share. Throughout this book you'll discover their responses to issues such as identity in Christ, family dilemmas, postmodernism, peer pressure, dating, maintaining a healthy weight, clothing choices, and how it's possible to be a Christian and still be cool. You'll also receive my girlfriendly advice and biblically based commentary every step of the way. My goal is to direct you toward God's immeasurable love for you and His desire to help you succeed in all areas of your life.

To be a follower of Christ is the most rewarding experience you'll ever encounter, but it's also a challenge to take a stand and be set apart from the rest of the world (see Romans 12:2). Everyone who is a Christian has experienced hardships along the way, but having Jesus (and other Christian friends) in your life means you don't have to go it alone.

That's why I wanted to provide you with this book. When I was your age, I would have appreciated the opportunity to read about others' struggles and experiences. I would have benefited from getting some advice and a fresh perspective on what I cared about, but I wasn't aware of any such books at the time.

Times have changed! In this book you'll hear from plenty of people who understand what you're up against and want to help you achieve victory. Hey, you're not alone—we're in this together. So read on, and let's discover what it means to take our talk and make it walk.

How to Be a Winner

Check it out:

Proverbs 3:5-6

Would you like to know the secret of success? I'm not talking about how to acquire cash, cool cars, and designer clothes. If success were defined by the things we own, then Paris, Nicole, Lindsay, and Britney would all be respectable role models. No. When I mention success, I'm referring to a genuine sense of fulfillment that comes not from the outside but from the depths of the soul.

Every girl desires to feel good about herself, but what happens when she bases her contentment on something temporary like physical attractiveness, popularity, money, or fame? Well, it's no secret that money can't buy happiness, and as far as good looks are concerned, the Bible teaches that "beauty is fleeting" (Proverbs 31:30). Fame and social status are shaky too. I could give you a list of celebs, beginning with Marilyn Monroe right up to Anna Nicole Smith, who discovered that fame didn't bring the satisfaction they craved. In fact, the success of those two beautiful women was short-lived, ending in tragic drug overdoses.

A friend and I were shopping in a clothing store recently

and couldn't help but feel disturbed about some of the products that were on display. The store featured drinking games, sexually inspired books, and T-shirts with disturbing messages on the front. One read "I Live for Kicks" and another, "Pleasure Victim." Think about it. Those messages encourage you to believe that life is all about getting satisfaction from the world through fun and pleasure, but that's a straight-up lie! Living for "kicks" won't amount to anything substantial. It's just short-term gratification—a way to feel good for a little while.

The world will tell you to rush after your passion to find happiness, but after you've obtained it and the fairy dust settles, you will still have emptiness of soul and spirit. Having money in the bank, credit cards, and a hot body won't give you a real sense of purpose. The only way you can obtain lasting fulfillment is through someone who is not of this world—the Lord Jesus Christ! Only He can help you achieve the kind of success that endures.

You may have heard of the '90s rock group Nirvana. The lead singer was Kurt Cobain, and if anyone appeared to have it all, it was this former teen idol. Cobain had screaming fans around the globe, and his albums sold millions. He'd won awards and Grammys, and had earned more money than he could spend. In addition to all this fame, he had an adorable baby daughter. There wasn't one thing the world had to offer that Kurt Cobain hadn't obtained. Yet in 1994, he ended his life with a gunshot. Why? From a worldly perspective it didn't make sense, but from a spiritual viewpoint, it came into sharp focus. Without a relationship with Jesus Christ, Kurt Cobain didn't have peace and contentment. He might have felt the temporary rush of newfound success, but once the excitement wore off, he was still surrounded by everything he despised, including himself. He was so discontented, in fact, that he chose to abandon it all and take his own life.

Obviously, not every person who's not a follower of Christ will become suicidal, but there's something to be learned from Kurt Cobain's horrific death: a person can have everything and nothing at the same time.

Jesus said in John 10:10 (NKJV) that He came so you could have life and have it abundantly. That doesn't mean you're not going to suffer trials and times of sorrow. You may have already been there—I know I have had my share of tough times. But what sets you apart from people like Marilyn Monroe, Anna Nicole Smith, and Kurt Cobain is that even in the midst of heartache, you can experience the peace that passes all understanding (see Philippians 4:7, RSV). Your life can have meaning and purpose, regardless of whether or not you have everything you desire. That's the promise Jesus has given you!

In my own life, things haven't always turned out the way I planned or hoped. I know what it's like to suffer anguish and broken dreams, as I'll describe in a later chapter. But through my tears, I've clung to the knowledge that my sense of value isn't dependent on people or circumstances. During those difficult moments, I remembered that I belong to the Lord and my identity is rooted in Him. That assurance gave me strength to move forward and trust God's plan for my future, even when things weren't going my way.

Let's return to the question I asked at the beginning of this chapter: "Would you like to know the secret of success?" The answer is revealed in one of my favorite verses, Jeremiah 29:11: "'I know the plans I have for you,' declares the LORD, 'plans to prosper you and not to harm you, plans to give you hope and a future.'" If you're completely surrendered to God and if you follow His will, as revealed in the Bible, you cannot fail because He has already established the master plan for your life. Your obligation is to live it out. "We are God's workmanship, created in Christ Jesus to do good works, which God prepared in advance for us to do" (Ephesians 2:10).

To adhere to God's calling is to discover His purpose for your life. I can't suggest what His plans might be, but I *can* promise you they're more significant than anything you could envision on your own. And the best part is that whatever accomplishments you enjoy in life will bring glory and honor to Him.

Do you want to be a winner? Then "seek first his kingdom and his righteousness" (Matthew 6:33).

That's your formula for success!

LET'S TALK ABOUT SUCCESS

DUSTY SANDERSON (student, age 17): I think success is living your life according to God's plan and feeling like you've given all you can to Him. If you make God happy and please Him, then you please yourself. As far as my future is concerned, I'm considering becoming a pastor. I enjoy sharing the love of God with people who are lost—telling them what He's done for me and how He's changed my life.

MATT GODSHALL (student, age 14): I heard a pastor say that we sometimes think of our lives as our own story, with God just kind of thrown in. In reality, we are part of God's story.

ERIN DIEFENBACH (student, age 17): I'm trying to focus on what God wants me to do rather than on what I think I'm good at. If I parallel my life with His purposes, I believe

I'll be successful. Right now I think God's will for my future might be to become a marriage counselor because I enjoy encouraging my friends who come to me for advice. But I'm trying to stay open in case He has other plans. I think the best way to discover God's will is to talk to Him about everything and to read the Bible to find answers. God wants to be incorporated into our daily lives, so if we're paying attention to our circumstances and really trying to listen to Him, we'll eventually get a sense of direction.

CHRISTIAN TURNER *(student, age 16): I want to be part of something bigger than myself, so I'm excited to discover the plans God has for me. One of these days I'm going to be standing in eternity, and I'm going to have to answer for what I did with my life. I want to hear God tell me that I was a faithful servant. I wouldn't want Him to reveal the wonderful things I missed because I was too busy following my own ambitions. I want to have peace in knowing that I was faithful to my calling.*

PAUL HONTZ *(student, age 19): Success is the direct result of our obedience to God. Through Him we are made complete.*

ALYSON THOMAS *(student, age 16): As far as my future is concerned, I'm still in confusion mode. Right now I'm devoting a lot of prayer to this issue. I wish God would send me an e-mail with the words, "Thou shalt do this for thy future," but it's not that easy. I'm trusting that He will reveal His plan for my life at the right time.*

MARY SPAGNOLA *(student, age 16): So far, a lot of things I've wanted haven't turned out the way I'd hoped, but in hindsight they turned out better than I could have planned.*

I have faith that God knows what He's doing and that His ways are so much better than my own.

SARAH UTTERBACK *(student, age 16): I really want to become a chef. I'd like to go to a four-year college for hotel and restaurant management and then to culinary school. Eventually I'd like to open my own restaurant and catering service. As much as I want this dream for my life, I'm willing to submit to God's plan if it's different from my own. I'm trying to keep my heart and mind open to His will.*

MR. AUSTIN SEFTON *(youth leader): As far as my career is concerned, I don't know where God is going to use me. Right now I'm attending a community college, but I'm not sure what I'll major in. I'm spending a lot of time reading my Bible, praying, and asking God to reveal His plan for my life. Every Christian has a specific calling, and it's different for everybody. Once we discover where God wants to place us, then it's up to us to live it out in total surrender. The definition of success is to seek first the Kingdom of God and His righteousness (Matthew 6:33). Success is striving after His will and discovering our place in His Kingdom.*

PASTOR AUSTIN DUNCAN *(youth minister): Life may seem out of control for you at this stage of your life—your hormones are raging, you're making friends, you're losing friends, you're having issues with guys. But God is on His throne [Psalm 115:3], and if you love Him, then He is using every single circumstance—both good and bad—for your good and for His glory. Every one of us has issues with discontentment, but discontentment is really the temptation to complain against the sovereignty of God. He is in control of the universe and of your life, so you can draw comfort* from the fact that where He has you today is exactly where you're supposed to be.

MR. MATT NORTHRUP (high school dean): I think the definition of success is to look more like Christ today than you did yesterday. It's learning to sacrifice as Christ sacrificed, to serve as He served, and to love as He loved. ❀

What Say You?

1) What is *your* definition of success?

2) How do you think God defines success for your life?

3) What is the promise that Jesus has given you in John 10:10?

4) How can you discover God's plan and purpose for your life?

Got More than Milk?

Check it out:

Ephesians 4:13-15

One day I passed a camera shop and saw a large photo in the window of a one-year-old boy with cake all over his face and hands. The picture was meant to be cute. After all, the little guy was still a baby, and everyone expects a baby to smear frosting everywhere but in his mouth. But what if the photo had featured a grown man with cake all over himself? It wouldn't have been so cute. In fact, it would have been disgusting. If I had seen a photo like that in the store window, my first thought would have been, *Gross*!

Well, as sad as it is, some Christians stay at the "cake face" stage their entire lives. They never grow in their relationship with the Lord, and they're forever slipping back into their bad habits and then rebounding. In essence they remain infants, like the apostle Paul talked about in 1 Corinthians 3:1-3: "I could not address you as spiritual but as worldly—mere infants in Christ. I gave you milk, not solid food, for you were not yet ready for it. Indeed, you are still not ready. You are still worldly."

Does that sound like anyone you know? Do you have

Christian friends who are routinely getting caught up in worldly activities—things that would displease the Lord—and then asking Him for forgiveness? Do they seem uncomfortable when you talk about God or share a truth from the Bible? Is there evidence of rebellious behavior or attitudes that goes on for an extended period of time? If so, you might as well pop some pacifiers in their mouths and hand them some rattles, because they've stunted their spiritual growth.

Then there are those who advance to an adolescent stage in their relationship with the Lord and stay there permanently. That's as far as they go and as far as they'll grow. They remain at a high school level until they're seventy or eighty years old!

That's not what the Christian life is about. God never intended His children to reach one stage of spiritual growth and come to a screeching halt. He desires us to continually move forward in our relationship with Him and become more mature in our faith. In one of my favorite Scriptures the apostle Paul addresses this: "I do not consider myself yet to have taken hold of it. But one thing I do: Forgetting what is behind and straining toward what is ahead, I press on toward the goal to win the prize for which God has called me heavenward in Christ Jesus" (Philippians 3:13-14).

The Christian life is a journey, and all of us should be advancing with every turn. Think back to what your relationship with God was like one year ago. Have you grown closer to Him since then? Have you become more knowledgeable in His Word and more willing to be obedient? I heard a pastor say that we should be able to see evidence of spiritual growth in our lives from year to year. If not, then we need to sit down and seriously assess the reason(s) we haven't matured in faith. Sometimes it's because of unconfessed sin in our lives. At other times, it's because we haven't put enough effort into developing our relationship with the Lord. Someone once said, "If you haven't felt close to God lately, guess who moved?" Once you know the reason for your spiritual slump, you can begin to do something to remedy it.

When I was in college, I made the mistake of falling into the slump mode. Sure, I went to church and prayed when I needed God's help, but that was the extent of my effort. My main priorities were my studies and my friends—God was just one small part of my busy life. Then, in my mid-twenties, I got hit by a tidal wave of adversity. It seemed like everything that mattered to me went down the drain within one year. In the midst of all my pain and trauma, I began talking to the Lord every day and developing a relationship with Him. I knew it wasn't just a temporary fix to get me through my troubles; I had made a sincere commitment to stay close to God. More than a decade has passed since then, along with some intense heartaches and frustrations, but I'm pleased to say I've stayed true to that commitment. I've remained faithful. And although I'll always be a major project under construction by God, I've come a long way from point A!

How about you? Has your faith in God grown and matured in the past year, or have you been guilty of stagnating lately? Wherever you are on the spiritual growth chart, you can make a decision today to get to know God on a deeper level. It doesn't take a great deal of effort—just a commitment to be faithful in studying and obeying His Word and talking to Him through prayer.

Does your busy life make it difficult to spend time with

the Lord? That's an issue most of us struggle with periodically, but let's think about that for a moment. The God of the universe—Maker of heaven and earth, King of kings, and Lord of lords—wants to spend time with us one-on-one, and we can't seem to make it happen because we're too *busy*? There's something terribly wrong with that picture! We should be thanking Him every day that we have the privilege to come into His presence and get to know Him. The Lord longs to work in our lives and equip us for greater service, but we must first be willing to learn how to relate to Him. And that takes time.

In the beginning of this chapter, I described Christians who fail to grow in the Lord and consequently remain at the "cake face" stage their entire lives. I have full confidence that *you* won't be one of them! My assurance stems from the promise of Philippians 1:6, which says we can be "confident of this, that he who began a good work in you will carry it on to completion until the day of Christ Jesus." Just as God has helped me mature in my Christian life, He will do the same for you.

As you commit to spending time in fellowship with the Lord each day, He will fulfill His promise to do an amazing work in your life. You'll be astounded by the positive changes you see within yourself from year to year. You'll go from drinking only spiritual milk to digging in to the "meat" of the Word of God. That's what spiritual maturity is all about.

"Anyone who lives on milk, being still an infant, is not acquainted with the teaching about righteousness. But solid food is for the mature, who by constant use have trained themselves to distinguish good from evil" (Hebrews 5:13-14).

LET'S TALK ABOUT GROWING SPIRITUALLY

MR. AUSTIN SEFTON (youth leader): For the better part of my junior high and high school years, I wasn't interested in spending much time with the Lord. Had I done that, it would have benefited me in every area of my life. Right now I'm reading the book of John, and I'm coming across amazing teachings of Jesus that I hadn't noticed before. I've grown up in church my entire life, yet there's always something new to discover.

MARIN JOHNSEN (student, age 15): A lot of Christians in my generation are weak spiritually, which must be a total turnoff to nonbelievers. I think the Christians who have a true heart for God need to step up and take charge to a greater extent. They should become more assertive.

ERIN DIEFENBACH (student, age 17): I'm a strong believer in having accountability partners. I have one right now, and she really helps me in my spiritual walk. I think if you're going to have an accountability partner, it should be a Christian friend of your own gender who really knows you— including your faults—but won't judge or criticize you. Also, I know we're all super busy, but it's important to take time to talk to God and to really listen. To do that without interruption, we need to turn off the music and computers and just be still.

MARY SPAGNOLA (student, age 16): Every night I read devotions and my Bible. It's so encouraging because most of the time whatever I'm reading lines up with what I'm going through at the time. It's amazing how often that happens. I'm also actively involved in my youth group, which is great because I have lots of Christian friends. I have older

Christian people in my life as well, who serve as mentors and role models.

MR. AUSTIN SEFTON (youth leader): I would encourage every Christian to get involved in a Bible study—hopefully a group that's studying a book of the Bible. The best way to learn about God is straight from the source. We get our nutrients and spiritual food by hearing God speak to our hearts through His Word. Think of it as eating meat—the protein and nourishment we get from the meat is ultimately going to sustain our bodies. Gravy enhances the flavor of the meat, but nobody can live on gravy alone. In the same way, Christian books help explain and enhance what the Bible says, but the Word of God is where we should go for our spiritual nourishment. I'd also encourage you to read the Bible and pray on your own time. That's how the relationship between you and the Lord will come to life.

PASTOR JONATHAN LAKES (youth minister): One of the most important things I try to inspire people to do is ask questions. Searching for answers provides an opportunity for truth to reveal itself. I like to foster a safe environment within our youth group where kids can do that, as well as share their experiences and develop a closer walk with the Lord. I also encourage students to put themselves in other social circles where their spiritual development will be nurtured.

PASTOR AUSTIN DUNCAN (youth minister): There is nothing like a solid Christ-centered church! Jesus loved the church and died for it. He promised its success [Matthew 16:18], so when you're part of the church [the family of believers], you're part of something that is *indestructible and eternal. Of course, the most important thing you can do is give your life to Christ, but after doing that, it's essential to start living within the body of believers. God did not intend for us to be solo Christians. Hebrews 10:25 instructs us to not give up meeting together. It's essential not only to attend a church but to really become part of it—to have a pastor, to form friendships, to serve, and to be discipled and cared for. The church is a precious place—it's precious to God and it's precious to people.*

Do you have a friend who has stopped growing in his or her relationship with the Lord?

JENNA SALLADIN (student, age 17): I have a friend who's gone to church her entire life and has been fed Christianity, but she's not sure she believes everything she's been taught. She needs to spend quality time with God and really get to know Him.

ELISSA MASON (student, age 14): One of my friends started hanging out with nonbelievers at school, and now she doesn't come to church and youth group as much. When she does come, all she talks about is the drama that's going on in her life and who's going out with who.

CHRISTIAN TURNER (student, age 16): I have a friend who's been dating a non-Christian girl. Even though my friend is still coming to church, he's just going through the motions. I can't relate to him on a spiritual level anymore. He's become jaded and a lot more distant from other people. For lack of a better word, he's kinda fake.

BECCA YOUNKMAN (student, age 17): Sometimes people who you think have stopped growing in their faith were never growing to begin with. They may have gone to church and a Christian school, but they were just there. You need to try to help them.

What spiritual changes would you like to see within yourself one year from now?

JONATHAN YOUNKMAN (student, age 15): I'd like to become more involved in mission trips. For example, in December our church youth group takes shoe boxes of toys and necessities to Mexico to give to needy families.

BECCA YOUNKMAN (student, age 17): I'd like to form a better connection with God through prayer—not just saying words such as "Thank you for this beautiful day. Amen," but to really have deep conversations with the Lord. Another thing I'd like to improve on is absorbing the pastor's message on Sunday mornings. He says a lot of great things, but my mind wanders into la-la land, so I don't get much out of the sermons.

DAVID STRUM (student, age 15): I'd like to become open with friends about my Christian faith. In my youth group at church we talked about two types of evil people. There's the person who does evil, and there's the person who sees evil being committed and does nothing to stop it. At times I'm in the second category. My friends will talk about inappropriate things, and I'll turn away and won't say anything to discourage them. I need to work on becoming bolder in my stand for righteousness. One way to do that is to read my Bible more frequently. Right now I read a little in the mornings, but I'd like to study it in greater depth.

ELISSA MASON (student, age 14): I struggle with wanting

to control my life. Sometimes I'll be stressing about a school assignment and I won't think to stop and pray. I forget to bring God into my daily problems, so I'm going to change that.

MARIN JOHNSEN *(student, age 15): I'd like to be more consistent with my quiet times with God, and I'd also like to become more others-centered and less self-centered.* ✿

What Say You?

1) Do you know Christian friends or family members who have stopped growing in their relationship with the Lord? What do you think caused this lack of maturity? Can you think of something you might say or do to encourage them to get back on track? (It would be a good idea to seek guidance from the Lord beforehand.)

2) Write down three ways that you can help accelerate spiritual growth in your life.

3) What changes would you like to see within yourself one year from now?

Use It or Lose It

Check it out:

Matthew 25:14-30

When I was a kid, my dad used to drive my friends and me to school in our car pool. To pass the time during the twenty-minute trip, he often told us adventure stories he made up about interesting animal characters. Although we enjoyed every furry friend he invented, there was one character we loved more than any other—a dog named Woof. Now this pup wasn't a purebred or even very cute. He had a bent ear and a crooked leg and tail—not the type of dog most people want for a pet. But Woof was very smart and was always doing heroic deeds and getting into adventures, and that made him special in spite of his outward appearance.

The kids in our car pool *loved* to hear Dad tell Woof stories! In fact, I think he grew weary of our requests, because one morning he dropped us off at the front of the school and ended a story by saying that Woof had died! Would you believe we actually got depressed? After some tears and a mopey day at school, we talked Dad into resurrecting our imaginary friend. Phew! That was a close call.

With Woof still in the land of the living, I decided at the age of eleven to write my own story about this fun-loving pup. Encouraged by my parents, I took my pad and pencil (I didn't own a computer then) and wrote *Woof! A Bedtime Story about a Dog*. After some editorial tweaks from my dad, I submitted it to a Christian publishing company to see if they wanted to print it. They did, and I became an author at the age of twelve! To this day, I still hold the title of being the youngest author in that publishing company's fifty-seven-year history, which is one of God's greatest gifts to me.

Since that time, I've written nine more Woof adventures, along with some other children's books with different characters. I've also written two books for teen girls, one of which you're reading now. The reason I've shared my writing history with you is not to brag but to talk about the driving force behind my published manuscripts.

In order to understand how my career evolved, let's rewind to my earliest elementary school years. I used to enjoy creative writing assignments and would often bring them home to show to my parents. My mom and dad noticed that their daughter had a flair for writing and often complimented me on my style and imagination. With their support, I continued to express myself on paper until I eventually wrote my first Woof manuscript.

You may be thinking this is all well and good, but how does it relate to *you*? Good question. Here's the link: just as I've discovered a talent the Lord has given me, I know He has also given you at least one talent, or maybe even more! If you're unsure what your talent(s) might be, stop and ask yourself, *What am I good at? What do I enjoy doing? What can I do better than most people I know?*

The Bible says that as a follower of Christ, you are uniquely blessed with abilities that were given to you by God for His service. How many talents you've been given isn't what matters the most, though. The big question is, how are you using them?

You may recall Jesus' parable of the talents in Matthew 25. In that passage, he tells the story of a man who goes away and leaves a share of talents (a certain amount of money) to three servants. One servant was given five talents, a second servant was given two talents, and a third servant was given only one. Their master wanted them to use the talents while he was away to earn additional money. When he returned, he was very pleased to find that two of the servants had doubled the amount he had given them. But the third servant had foolishly buried his money in the ground and hadn't earned even one percent! The master was very angry with this man and called him "wicked" and "lazy." He punished that lazy servant severely for his negligence, and took the one talent from him and gave it to the servant who had earned the most.

The message in Jesus' parable of the talents isn't about wasting money—it's about wasting talents! Some Christians are too lazy or afraid to put their abilities to use; therefore, they displease God. They are wasting their talents, just like the wicked servant did when he hid his money in the ground.

Here's an example. My friend Andrew is what people would call a "nice Christian guy." Andrew goes to church, gives money regularly, and occasionally attends Bible studies and church events. I believe he loves the Lord, but as far as I can tell, he isn't doing anything in service for Him. I've talked to Andrew about the possibility of volunteering in some way or going on a mission trip, but he seems disinterested. What he *really* likes to do is check out Internet dating sites when he gets home from work. There's nothing wrong with that, but his priorities are out of balance. He doesn't seem to place any emphasis on developing and using his skills for the Lord.

How about you? Are you putting your talents to use? If not, let me encourage you to pray and ask God for direction. Ask your parents or teachers what they think you're good at. Then start focusing on how you can use your talents to help others and glorify the Lord. He has a job that's just right for you!

It's important to note that while we all have been given unique spiritual abilities, one person's talent isn't superior to someone else's talent. We're all part of the body of Christ (see 1 Corinthians 12:27), and each one of us has a significant role to play in God's Kingdom.

Perhaps the Lord may eventually call you to build a career around the talent He has given you, like He has done with my writing and speaking ministry. Or maybe you'll seek employment in the secular world while offering your services to your church in some way, such as singing, playing an instrument, providing meals for sick members, or helping with children's ministry. You might also volunteer your time and skills to a nonprofit organization that promotes a worthy cause such as feeding homeless people. I know a lot of people who are involved in serving others regularly, and they derive a great deal of fulfillment from it.

One of the rewards of being faithful to the Lord is that He often blesses you in return. For instance, when I volunteered at a camp for disabled children last summer, I didn't go there to receive anything—I wanted to serve. But by the end of the weekend I was blown away by all the gratification I received. To see little children wrapping their arms around my legs and looking up at me with sweet smiles was so uplifting! I came home refreshed and renewed.

Even if you don't receive immediate perks and benefits, serving God and knowing He's satisfied with your efforts is a tremendous blessing. It's a reward in itself. And the cool thing is, God doesn't miss anything you do for Him. Someday you'll receive rewards in heaven for your willing and humble service for Him on earth (see Matthew 16:27).

So how will you use *your* talents for your Lord and Master?

LET'S TALK ABOUT TALENTS

PASTOR LUKE CUNNINGHAM (youth minister): If you have a talent, make it known. God has given you that platform for a reason. One of the coolest things I've seen is an athlete who wears a symbol of his or her faith during a game or a tournament. I'm reminded of Tim Tebow (quarterback and Heisman Trophy winner), who wears John 3:16 on his face mask during football games. What an incredible testimony of his faith in Christ! Whenever Tebow's teammates talk about him, they always mention that he's a Christian. We had a kid in our youth group who was a cross-country runner, and he would compete with a cross displayed on each of his calves. How could anyone miss that? Even if you're not an athlete, you have an opportunity to use whatever talents you've been given to bring glory to God.

PASTOR AUSTIN DUNCAN (youth minister): Ephesians 5:15-16 talks about redeeming the time—using it in a way that honors God. That's hard to accomplish if you're playing video games eighteen hours a day. We are stewards of our time, our cash, and our talents. We need to be faithful with what we've been given.

JON SALLADIN (student, age 15): I feel like God has gifted me in public speaking, so I really want to become a pastor. I've already received the call from the Lord to begin preparing for that. For now, I'm playing guitar in my church's worship band, and I also try to be a Christian example in the sports I play.

BECCA YOUNKMAN (student, age 17): I have an artistic side and I'm into photography. I've thought about going to a mission field in South Central Europe and getting a job where I could use my photography skills.

ELISSA MASON (student, age 14): I enjoy doing ballet and lyrical dancing. I'm going on a mission trip in two weeks, and my church has asked me to dance in a musical they're putting together. I'm really excited about that! In regard to my future, I want to do something that involves caring for people, such as nursing. I feel drawn to Africa, so I'd enjoy doing some kind of medical missions work there.

BEN TRAPP (student, age 15): I enjoy working with children. Last year I went on a mission trip with a group from our church to visit kids at an AIDS camp. We were cautious at first for health reasons, but soon the fear barrier was broken and we were able to reach out in love to those underprivileged children. It was amazing! In two weeks I'll be going to the Bahamas on another mission trip, and I'm really looking forward to that.

JENNA SALLADIN (student, age 17): I sing and play bass in *our worship team at church, and I'd like to continue doing that for years to come.*

DAVID STRUM *(student, age 15): God has given me the ability to act and to play the guitar. Right now I perform with the worship band at my church. I'd also like to get involved with some form of drama ministry, like the Lighthouse Theater. They've done productions based on Bible stories and Christian books, such as The Lion, the Witch and the Wardrobe.* ❀

What Say You?

1) Can you name a talent God has given you?

2) Describe a time when you used your talent(s) for the Lord.

3) In what ways would you like to use your God-given abilities in the future?

4) Is there something you can do at this point in your life to prepare for greater service? Why not take a moment right now to ask the Lord about this? Jot down any thoughts that come to your mind.

Smart Money

Check it out:

Hebrews 13:5

I remember the thrill like it was yesterday. I was fifteen years old and had just returned home from a ski trip in Mammoth Mountain, California. As I flipped through the mail that night, I came across a letter from a book club that took my breath away. Across the front of the envelope in bold letters were these words: "DANAE DOBSON! $10,000 WINNER!" I ripped it open and scanned the form letter (which should have served as a red flag in and of itself). The confirmation was as clear as a bell, at least to this financially strapped student: "CONGRATULATIONS, DANAE DOBSON!!! You are the *guaranteed** winner of $10,000.00!!! Reply at once!!!"

Me?! A $10,000 winner? I reread the letter again and again. There was no mistaking it—Danae Dobson had indeed won ten grand!

I'm not sure why I didn't bother mentioning my newfound fortune to my parents (perhaps on a subconscious level I suspected they'd pop my balloon). Instead, I took the news to a select group of people I knew would be elated for me: my peers. The next day at school

I announced to my close friends (and a few acquaintances who sat next to me in my classes): "Guess what? I've won $10,000!" Word quickly spread throughout the halls of my high school campus, much to my surprise and delight. Pretty soon I was being approached by students I knew and some I hadn't met before, all wanting to know the answer to the same question: "Did you really win ten grand?" A Cheshire cat–like grin would spread across my face each time I confirmed that yes, what they had heard was correct. I was a winner—*winner*—WINNER!

One friend even asked if he could borrow five hundred dollars for a drum set. He promised to give my little brother, Ryan, drum lessons if I would grant his request. I had to hold in my laughter as he said with enthusiasm, "I can teach him rhythm and beat!"

Long story short, I gleefully contacted the book club (not Publishers Clearing House, but a similar operation) to cash in on my big money, only to find that my "prize" wasn't anything that resembled green paper with U.S. presidents on the front. I went back to that cherished form letter and studied it, this time searching for loopholes. Sure enough, a few subtle twists like "may," "could," and "*" took the guarantee out of the *guarantee.**

So what did I do about the publicity swirling around my high school campus? Well, I was too embarrassed to reveal I'd been gullible, so I chose to handle the situation the best way I knew how as a fifteen-year-old: I kept my mouth shut and let it play itself out. I never gave anyone a full explanation of what happened to my supposed jackpot, which is why there's a statement in my yearbook, penned by a friend who drew a smiley face and wrote: "$10,000? I want proof!"

Chalk it up to another lesson in life. These days I don't

give a second thought to gimmicks surrounding cash and prizes. Whenever I receive a sweepstakes notification in the mail, I toss it in the trash unopened. The same goes for computer-generated messages on my telephone answering machine that promise trips to Hawaii, Tahiti, or the Caribbean. They get deleted after the first sentence or two. Whoever made up the slogan "There's no such thing as a free lunch" must have lived it. I know I have!

First Timothy 6:9 says, "People who want to get rich fall into temptation and a trap and into many foolish and harmful desires that plunge men into ruin and destruction." Do you know anyone who fits that profile? There are a few people who come to my mind, like the woman I know who lost $2,500 playing Internet poker, or the man who invested most of his savings in a get-rich-quick scheme that went belly-up, or the homeless man I've witnessed buying lottery tickets at the convenience mart, hoping to hit the mega-money jackpot. All these folks were enticed by the lure of easy money.

Does the Lord prohibit you from becoming wealthy through reasonable endeavors? No. There are many characters in the Bible whom He blessed with great riches—the wealthiest being King Solomon. Amazing thing is, Solomon never asked for riches; he asked for wisdom, so guess what God gave him? Wisdom *and* riches. Throughout his lifetime, he had no equal among kings (see 1 Kings 3:13; 4:30). Just how wealthy was Solomon? This will give you an idea: each year he received a minimum of twenty-five tons of gold. He also had twelve thousand horses (see 1 Kings 10:14, 23-26)! Now that's a lot of thundering hooves!

So what's the harm in being rich? Jesus taught that it's not the accumulation of, but rather the *love* of, money that causes a person's downfall. He profoundly stated in Matthew 6:24, "No one can serve two masters. Either he will hate the one and love the other, or he will be devoted to the one and despise the other. You cannot serve both God and Money." What message does that say to you? For me, it comes down to priorities. Money is important, but I need to keep the desire for it under control, as well as the spending.

One of the ways I keep in check materially is by applying the principle of giving 10 percent of my earnings to God through tithes and offerings.

In 2 Corinthians 9:7 we are told that "God loves a cheerful giver." He desires for us to share our money with the church and with those in need—not out of obligation, but with a willing and joyful spirit. Sharing what we have keeps our priorities in balance and our materialistic urges in check. It is also a way of acknowledging to the Lord that He has control of our finances.

Have you considered that God owns everything you have? It's true. The Bible says that "The earth is the LORD's, and everything in it, the world, and all who live in it" (Psalm 24:1). That means that all the things you possess—your computer, your music, your movies, your jewelry, your clothes, and your shoes—were purchased with God's money. Everything you have is on loan from Him; you are a steward of all He has entrusted to you.

The truth is that every spending decision is a spiritual decision. When I was in elementary school, I once threw a perfectly good sandwich in the trash because I felt like eating junk food that day. I immediately felt a little guilty. In hindsight, I can see that my conscience was pricked, not just because I was wasting food, but because I was squandering what belonged to the Lord. Every blessing is a gift from His hand.

Ever heard of the phrase "Lord of *all* or not at all"? When it comes to your finances—and everything else, for that matter—you need to relinquish total control to God. That's a basic principle of Scripture, and you can't go wrong by abiding by it. You will discover again and again that it pays (in much greater ways than cash!) to keep the Lord at the center of your life. Every time. All the time.

So go ahead and pursue your financial interests, but remember to exercise control and pray for wisdom. And, hey—take a nugget from this former "fool's gold" subscriber: if you get one of those lame sweepstakes notifications in the mail, stash it where it belongs—in the nearest trash can!

"Whoever loves money never has money enough; whoever loves wealth is never satisfied with his income. This too is meaningless" (Ecclesiastes 5:10; written by King Solomon, the wealthiest and wisest man in history!).

LET'S TALK ABOUT MONEY

PASTOR AUSTIN DUNCAN (youth minister): Most teens are "burners" with their money—they get it and then it's gone. They consider money to be a renewable resource, and unfortunately that backfires on them when they end up with a heap of credit card debt in college. Wouldn't it be better if they learned about that danger at an earlier age so they could avoid it? God cares about our money because it belongs to Him. Did you know that there are 1,500 to 2,000 Scriptures in the Bible on the topic of money? In the same way that we're stewards of our speech, we are stewards of the resources He's given us. In Randy Alcorn's book

The Treasure Principle, *he says that whenever he buys something, he imagines it sprouting wings and flying away. He understands the reality that all our material possessions are temporal.*

JON SALLADIN (student, age 15): I tithe 10 percent of my income, and I don't compromise on that. My family donates money to our church, to poor people, and to missionaries. We also support a kid in Africa. My spending cash goes toward sports equipment and shoes—I love Vans and Converse brands!

ALYSON THOMAS (student, age 16): I'm not earning any money right now, so I can't tithe regularly. However, tithing isn't the only way to honor God with our money. Good stewardship is important too. We should know when it's the right time to save, spend, or splurge. And we shouldn't spend money we don't have, like some people do by using credit cards to buy things they can't afford.

PAUL HONTZ (student, age 19): I try to manage my finances responsibly. I had the opportunity to live in Africa for several months, and it really changed my perspective on money.

PASTOR LUKE CUNNINGHAM (youth minister): My wife and I give 10 percent of everything we earn because it's biblical to do so. In Malachi 3:8 God says, "Will a man rob God? Yet you rob me. But you ask, 'How do we rob you?' In tithes and offerings." It doesn't get more plain than that. You have an obligation to give a percentage of your earnings back to God. So if you earn ten bucks, I recommend you give a dollar. If you earn one hundred, then give ten. By choosing to honor the Lord and put Him first in everything, including your finances, He's going to bless you.

Does that mean He'll give you a load of cash? Probably not. God's blessings aren't always financial—some are spiritual, such as peace and comfort. But if you're not giving God a percentage of your income, you're withholding what belongs to Him, and consequently causing Him to withhold from you. ❀

What Say You?

1) Where does the hazard lie in regard to money (see Matthew 6:24)?

2) What can happen to people who get caught in the snare of wanting to become rich (see 1 Timothy 6:9)?

3) How important is money to you? Rate your answer on a scale of 1 to 5 (with 1 being "not important" and 5 being "extremely important"). Consider your answer carefully and talk to the Lord about it.

4) Do you tithe 10 percent or more of the money you earn? Why does God want you to give?

Upgraded Version

Check it out:

Matthew 6:33

To the casual observer, fourteen-year-old Dylan seems like a nice guy. He goes to church regularly with his parents. He's a leader in his youth group. He's on the high school baseball team. He has a 4.0 grade point average. Yes, Dylan appears to be a model kid, but he writes and posts some of the filthiest things you could imagine on his MySpace page. His site is loaded with sexual content, crude humor, and foul language.

Recently his friend's mom saw the printed evidence. It wasn't hard to discover because Dylan's page was on display for the entire Web world to behold. She informed his parents, but when they confronted Dylan he denied the accusation, stating he didn't write anything inappropriate. Now Dylan's mad at his friend, as well as his friend's mom, and refuses to speak to them.

As I'm sure you're already aware, Dylan's obscene MySpace page is not uncommon (although it should not be the norm for a guy who goes to church and serves in the youth group). One girl told me she's been "horrified" by some of the content she has read on MySpace. Perhaps you, too, have been appalled by the written material and photos your peers have posted.

Social networking sites such as MySpace, Facebook, Friendster, and Orkut are great tools for connecting with friends, but unfortunately not everyone who uses them does so with discretion. There are those like Dylan who view MySpace as an opportunity to exploit themselves and their vulgar content to anyone who happens to stumble upon it. That's especially disturbing because MySpace is a widely used forum, with millions of people logging on daily. Just how popular is it? A recent statistic reports that if MySpace were a country, it would be the eleventh largest in the world!

MySpace may be the biggest social networking site, but it's not the only one. Christians have stepped into the virtual community too, with sites such as YourChristianSpace, MyPraize, Xianz, DittyTalk, and Christianster. These interactive alternatives are a great way for you to connect with other people who share your Christian faith and values.

Social networking sites are just one aspect of the Internet that requires discretion. Although the Web has enhanced our lives by providing the convenience of a virtually limitless supply of knowledge at our fingertips, it has also introduced age-inappropriate information, indecent YouTube videos, and easy access to pornography. Even innocent children searching for "toys" on the Internet will sometimes end up with "sex toys" on their computer screens.

Everywhere we turn we're bombarded with vulgarity, and not just online. We get it through books, music, movies, billboards, and TV shows. When you consider how much time we devote to entertainment, it becomes even more alarming.

According to a generational study by Jenna Reith, a

researcher with the American Counseling Association, most people ages thirteen to eighteen spend an average of six hours per day in front of a TV, movie, or computer screen. Can you relate to that? If you don't know how many hours you spend with electronic entertainment, here's a challenge. Add up the hours you spend in front of a TV or computer each day for the next seven days, then multiply that number by four, and you'll have the number of hours you spend in "screen time" for one month. Multiply that number by twelve and you'll have the hours you spend on such entertainment in a year. You might be surprised at the result. With so much time devoted to the media, the need for discernment intensifies, which begs the question, "Are we honoring the Lord in our choice of entertainment?"

A while back a friend sent me an e-mail informing me that she had seen the movie *Sex and the City*. She explained that she "didn't have peace" about going to the film beforehand, but she was with a group of her friends who had already bought her a ticket. In her e-mail, she complained about the raunchy plot lines, describing one that glamorized a homosexual kiss. I was thinking, *Duh! What did you expect from a movie with a name like* Sex and the City? *A Jane Austen theme? The title and the R rating are dead giveaways that the film holds nothing back.*

I e-mailed my friend back and gently suggested that she didn't have peace about watching the movie because the Holy Spirit had spoken to her conscience. I also reminded her of Psalm 101:3, which says, "I will set before my eyes no vile thing."

If a group of my friends had bought me a ticket to *Sex and the City*, I would have politely said, "Thank you very much for the offer, but I'm not comfortable seeing that movie. Would you mind if I get the ticket refunded? I'll just catch you guys later." I don't think anyone would have been offended by my decision, but even if all of my friends disagreed, I would still want to do what was right. My conviction might even cause someone else to think twice about going.

Obviously a movie like *Sex and the City*, with its homosexual kiss and all, is far from being considered wholesome entertainment. If my friend had asked the Lord for permission to see that movie beforehand, I seriously doubt that He would have answered, "Absolutely! You have my blessing. Don't forget the popcorn!" Everyone is born with a conscience and has the ability to discern right from wrong. In addition, all people who have placed their trust in Christ have been given the mind of Christ (see 1 Corinthians 2:16). If we don't have peace about a certain movie, book, or TV show, it's most likely because the Lord is instructing us to avoid it. He wants us to exercise discretion and keep our minds pure.

Is that burdensome? It doesn't have to be. In my own experience, I've seen a variety of cinematic hits that were morally uplifting, and I haven't had to skimp on great entertainment because I was selective. Quite the opposite.

One rule that I've established for myself is that unless a film is historical, I will not attend an R-rated movie. I made that decision years ago after attending some R-rated films that bothered me for a number of reasons. Some of the films had foul language and scenes that were so disturbing that my mind kept revisiting them. I finally arrived at the decision (most likely Spirit led) that I would no longer see an R-rated film unless it was historically based. There is also a small percentage of PG-13 films I choose to avoid, as well.

In most cases, the preview is enough to let me know which movies are full of sex, crude humor, and images that will pollute my mind.

One of the more troubling aspects of the entertainment industry is how often Christianity is made fun of in movies. Jesus is our Savior and best friend—it's upsetting to see Him mocked or hear His name raked through the gutter. The same is true for our heavenly Father. One of my friends told me that she went to see a movie and was distressed to hear one of the characters call God a filthy name. My friend told me, "At that moment, it was like someone poured a bucket of cold water over my head. I lost interest in the film, and I walked out."

Maybe that strikes a chord with you, as well. Have you ever heard or seen something so upsetting that you actually grieved? I have, and unfortunately I still remember it years later.

Philippians 4:8 says, "Whatever is true, whatever is noble, whatever is right, whatever is pure, whatever is lovely, whatever is admirable—if anything is excellent or praiseworthy—think about such things." It's hard to concentrate on things that are "right" if we're polluting our minds with trashy romance novels, Internet obscenities, and movies that celebrate promiscuity, foul language, and other forms of evil. As the popular saying goes, "garbage in, garbage out."

We have a responsibility as followers of Christ to "keep [ourselves] from being polluted by the world" (James 1:27). Is that possible in this high-tech age when so much of our time is devoted to cell phones, iPods, and computers?

Without question, the answer is yes. That's because what God told us in His Word more than two thousand years ago is still relevant today: "Do not conform any longer to the pattern of this world, but be transformed by the renewing of your mind. Then you will be able to test and approve what God's will is—his good, pleasing and perfect will" (Romans 12:2).

When we surrender to the Lord and give Him control of every area of our lives, we discover the awesome satisfaction that comes from communing with Him and being filled with His Spirit.

Nothing this virtual world has to offer can compare to that.

LET'S TALK ABOUT ENTERTAINMENT

PASTOR LUKE CUNNINGHAM (youth minister): I always tell teenagers, "Don't get used to ungodliness." I was at a conference recently where parents in the audience were shown a clip of a commercial for The Real World *on MTV. In the ad, the character Tila Tequila was talking about whether she should sleep with a man or a woman. The ad also featured two girls from* The Real World *who were cussing and making accusations such as, "You slept with him!" When the commercial was over, the parents in the auditorium were absolutely stunned. They were looking around the room and wondering, Is this really on TV? Are kids really watching this? Later, when teens were shown the same commercial, they were completely unmoved. Their response was, "Oh yeah, I've seen that. No big deal." That's because they had become used to ungodliness. When you hear a cuss word, it should ring a bell in your ear and make you say, "Whoa! What did I just hear?" When you're watching a TV show and they're talking garbage, it should sound an alarm in your mind. If it doesn't, then you've become desensitized. Remember the computer saying "GIGO" (garbage in,* garbage out)? If you get a virus in your computer, it's going to mess it up. In the same way, if you choose to pollute your mind, then you're a product of what you expose yourself to.

REBECCA YOUNG (student, age 16): I did a debate in my English class on the topic "Should the media be censored due to its portrayal of violence, drugs, and sexual behavior?" I argued in favor of it, and I made the point that the images we see stick in our minds, and we are influenced by them.

JONATHAN YOUNKMAN (student, age 15): Why not play board games with friends or family members on a weekend night instead of renting movies and going on the Internet?

BEN TRAPP (student, age 15): In my Latin class last Friday the teacher showed a movie with nude women in it—not just a short clip, but a long scene, and I've been considering talking to the principal about it. I was thinking, I didn't sign an agreement to view this stuff. It was unacceptable. As far as my personal selections, I log on to **Plugged In Online** (http://www.pluggedinonline.com) to find out about a film before I see it. If I read a description that says, "For mature audiences only" or if I find out that Christianity is made fun of, then I don't see it. I get enough flack for my Christian faith at school.

MATT GODSHALL (student, age 14): My standards revolve around sexual purity, so I incorporate that into my entertainment. Obviously, if I'm going to try to avoid checking out a girl who's walking down the street, then I'm not going to want to watch a movie that has sex scenes. That would be counterproductive. I can't escape every inappropriate scene, though, and there have been times when I've literally covered my eyes.

SARAH UTTERBACK *(student, age 16): Instead of wasting time filling our minds with garbage on TV or the Internet, why not spend a half hour reading our Bibles, praying to God, or spending time with a Christian friend?*

DUSTY SANDERSON *(student, age 17): On my school baseball team I hear a lot of guys talk about viewing porn like it's no big deal—kinda like, "Everybody does it."*

ERIN DIEFENBACH *(student, age 17): I gave a friend the riot act when I saw that he had pornographic stuff on his computer. Porn kills the mind. I know people who have looked at porn, and now they have unrealistic expectations about sex because their minds have become distorted.*

DAVID STRUM *(student, age 15): Some of the video games that my friends play are inappropriate, such as Grand Theft Auto. They'll ask me to play and I'll say, "Thank you, but that's not my kind of game." There's also certain types of movies that I won't see, and I won't use the Internet unless I'm researching for a school paper or watching YouTube. With YouTube, though, I never look up a general idea because approximately 30,000 videos show up on that site every week from all over the world. Nobody can regulate that efficiently. I like to view videos from sites where the clips have been reviewed ahead of time. As far as books are concerned, if I'm reading and I come to an unexpected inappropriate part, I'll skip twenty pages ahead and slowly work my way back. That way I can avoid the junk but not miss what I want to read.*

SARAH UTTERBACK *(student, age 16): When I was in third grade I wanted to write a letter to the president, so I clicked on a Web site that had the White House name in it, and* *all this porn popped up! I was horrified! It's like Satan finds ways to make us stumble upon it unintentionally. I think we should have a plan to click the "X" box immediately if porn pops up. There should be no hesitation.*

ALYSON THOMAS *(student, age 16): I have an image-based imagination, so when I see a raunchy scene on TV, I have to change the channel or it will stay in my mind for days. As far as using the Internet, I limit myself to e-mail, one or two Web sites, and nothing else. On the Google site they offer blockers, and I use them whenever I research a topic so I don't stumble onto anything inappropriate.*

MRS. FRANCES LEAF *(high school psychologist): It's wise to not "chat" with people you don't know on the Internet. You might have friends online who tell you they're in your age group, when in fact they are thirty-year-old men. In our home, computers are in the family room where we all hang out. I would never allow my kids to have computers in their bedrooms with no parental access. One of the boys I've worked with in counseling had porn issues with a couple of animated sites. This boy had to receive a great deal of therapy both in and out of school because of his addiction and other problems. When he was on campus, we made sure he had no access to computers, and he was escorted to his classes by a teacher's aide so he wouldn't stray. He ended up transferring to another school within our district that was more structured, which catered to his needs.*

SAMANTHA BOWSER *(student, age 17): Personally I have never been to an inappropriate Web site. In my family the computer is in the living room for a good reason, and the same is true for the TV—I'm not allowed to have a television* *in my bedroom. My mom wants to know what I'm watching, and she also wants me to be social.*

FRANKIE OGAZ *(student, age 16): Most TV programs aren't going to lead you toward God, unless they're holy reality shows, and I have yet to find one. Maybe the TV producers should create Bible Jeopardy.*

PASTOR AUSTIN DUNCAN *(youth minister): If Jesus Christ is Lord of your life, then He's the Lord of all of your life, including your entertainment. For instance, it's easy to think that songs on the radio are okay as long as they don't have cuss words (or the cuss words have been muted), but if the philosophy of the songs is in direct opposition to the cause of Christ, they're still unacceptable. If you mindlessly fill your life with unwholesome content, then Christ is not Lord of your entertainment. Reverend John MacArthur has a great quote that applies to this principle: "Worldliness is the failure to reject everything that appeals to the sin nature."* ❀

What Say You?

1) What will you do if a program or movie you're watching suddenly turns offensive?

2) Describe a time when you felt spiritually convicted regarding your choice of entertainment.

3) What standards have you established to keep yourself from being polluted by the world (see James 1:27)?

4) How would you respond if a friend encouraged you to view an inappropriate movie or Web site?

Nothing but the Truth

Check it out:

John 8:32

Recently I attended a party and began conversing with a girl I hadn't met before. I assumed she was a Christian because, well, it was a "Christian event." My mistake. When I casually mentioned praying about a decision, I was startled when she grinned and said, "That's great that you've found your spirituality. We all need to discover our individual meaning of religion." She went on to talk about guardian angels and showed me a green angel tattoo on her wrist. Then she drew my attention to a ring on her finger that had a mystical symbolism. As she talked, I kept hearing the word *religion* and how she believed it was necessary for all people—Muslims, Hindus, Buddhists, etc.—to find their personal version.

Suddenly I had a springboard to get personal myself. I said, "Do you know what I love most about my Christian faith? It's not about religion; it's about a relationship!" I went on to share that because of Jesus, I can pray to God about whatever I'm concerned about and know He's listening. I explained that He doesn't always answer my prayers according to my wishes, but the Bible assures me He's working everything out for my good. I concluded by saying that my relationship with the Lord is the most important part of my life.

Can you guess what this girl said in response? Nothing, really. She stood there smiling and nodding, and said something like, "That's great." What else could she say? As far as I could tell, I had just shot a hole through her understanding of Christianity. She probably had never equated a personal relationship with God to Christianity before. To her, it was just another religion or form of spirituality. After I left the party, I prayed that the Lord would break through the girl's confusion and provide more opportunities for "seeds of truth" to be planted in her mind. I also prayed that she would discover her own relationship with God through the saving power of His Son, Jesus Christ. Only then would she discover the real meaning of spiritual truth!

Let's talk about that concept for a moment. When I say the word *truth*, what comes to your mind? If words like *definite*, *concrete*, *right*, *absolute*, *factual*, *precise*, and *genuine* pop into your head, you're right. Truth is all of those things. But there's one word—actually, a name—that embodies truth: Jesus. That is the deeper meaning. How do I know this as fact? Because Jesus said so Himself! These are His words in John 14:6: "I am the way and the truth and the life. No one comes to the Father except through me."

You might think nobody would argue with Jesus' claim of being the absolute truth, but our society is full of people— even supposed Christians—who have subscribed to the idea of relativism, which claims there is *no* absolute truth.

David Brickner wrote an excellent article in a Jews for Jesus newsletter entitled "Truth Decay," in which he compares song lyrics from two artists who wrote forty years apart. Consider the following lyrics from a song called "Belief" by John Mayer:

We're never gonna win the world . . .
we're never gonna beat this
if belief is what we're fighting for.

Four decades ago a different John (Lennon) wrote a song called "Imagine" with a similar message:

Imagine there's no heaven . . .
Imagine all the people
living for today . . .

Dreaming, imagining, living without a belief system—without God, actually—is depressing; aren't you glad the Bible contradicts this nonsense? In another section of John Mayer's song, he talks about how belief is a beautiful armor, but it becomes the heaviest sword. By that statement he's saying that truth might look pretty, but it's burdensome. Well, here's some news for John Mayer: Scripture tells us that the Bible "is living and active." It is "sharper than any double-edged sword" (Hebrews 4:12). In other words, the power of the Word of God reaches into our innermost being and judges the thoughts and attitudes of the heart. How's that for a hefty dose of truth?

That's what I love about the Bible. There's no celebration of spiritual diversity in Scripture—no tolerance of sinful choices or debate over what's right or wrong. It's as solid as a five-ton rock! You can build a foundation of faith upon the Bible and know with assurance that it will stand against all opposition.

To look outside the Word of God for answers to life's questions is to rationalize anything, and I do mean *any-thing.* You may have already encountered this relativism in the classroom or among your circle of friends. Perhaps you've heard people arguing that there are no rules—nothing is moral or immoral, and anything goes. Maybe you've heard someone say that truth is relative—it's whatever *you* think it is.

David Brickner also wrote about a scene from the movie *Fiddler on the Roof* that underscores the concept of relativism. In the film, Tevye the milkman has a conversation with a few other fellow Jews regarding the problems of the world. One man remarks, "Why should I break my head about the outside world? Let the outside world break its own head!" "He is right," Tevye responds. "If you spit in the air, it lands in your face." Another man argues, "Nonsense, you cannot be blind to what happens outside!" "You know, he is also right." Tevye agrees. Frustrated, a fourth man points to the others and says, "He is right and he is right; they can't both be right!" Tevye looks at him and says, "You know, you are also right."

That's a lighthearted illustration, but it speaks to a greater issue. When the God of the universe and His Word are disregarded, every form of evil can be rationalized. That's what we're seeing in our culture right now—people ignoring biblical truths and creating their own forms of spirituality. The result has been a growing acceptance of every kind of sin.

Despite this trend toward moral relativism, people are continuing to crave meaning in their lives. That's why Rick Warren's book *The Purpose Driven Life* has sold more than 35 million copies! Everyone wants to have a purpose, but how can they achieve it with no belief system? It's like trying to walk on quicksand!

I'm reminded of a hymn chorus I've always liked:

On Christ the solid rock I stand,
All other ground is sinking sand,
All other ground is sinking sand.

A foundation built upon eternal truth will never be moved or shaken (Matthew 7:24-25). Now that's something to believe in!

As we can see in Matthew 7:24-27, the kind of foundation our lives are built upon is important: "Everyone who hears these words of mine and puts them into practice is like a wise man who built his house on the rock. The rain came down, the streams rose, and the winds blew and beat against that house; yet it did not fall, because it had its foundation on the rock. But everyone who hears these words of mine and does not put them into practice is like a foolish man who built his house on sand. The rain came down, the streams rose, and the winds blew and beat against that house, and it fell with a great crash."

LET'S TALK ABOUT TRUTH

ALYSON THOMAS (student, age 16): People talk about tolerance all the time. Yes, we do need to be kind and loving; however, the Bible says that some things are clearly evil. There's no doubt about that. Some truths are absolute. We have to accept that some people are going to think we're narrow-minded, and they might look at us funny and talk behind our backs, but Jesus said we're supposed to be a lamp on a stand and a city on a hill [Matthew 5:14-15]. If we're saying and doing what's right, then nothing can separate us from the love of Christ.

ERIN DIEFENBACH (student, age 17): *There is such a thing as absolute truth, and God made that clear in His Word. If anyone is unsure, just read the Bible more. It will confirm it.*

MR. AUSTIN SEFTON (youth leader): *The big thing now is to be open-minded. Some Christians think they can't give anyone scriptural advice for fear of offending, but Jesus was very confrontational in a loving way. With the woman at the well [John 4], Jesus told her that what she was doing was wrong.*

MRS. MEGAN BARBER (middle school teacher): *In my classroom, some students have no conscience about doing things such as lying to a parent, cheating on a test, or copying homework. They have no sense of right or wrong. They're living in an era that says, "You do what you want and I'll do what I want, and hopefully we'll work it out."*

MR. TIMOTHY STRANSKE (high school teacher): *Postmodernism is definitely impacting the way kids think— or don't think at all. In my class, when students have done assignments related to moral issues, such as biotechnology, they think all they need to do is give their opinion and then they're done. Many of the students' answers are related to what they've heard in movies. It's difficult to have a discussion when there's nothing to compare and contrast, and no standard to analyze. When people have an "anything goes" mind-set, it causes them to become intellectually lazy. They just have random thinking that they make up as they go along. Another thing I've noticed is that students sometimes change their positions based on their own self-interests. What seems like a good idea today might be a bad idea tomorrow if it's no longer useful to them.*

MR. WILLIAM ZUETEL (middle school teacher): It's unfortunate that Christian teachers who work in public schools are often not allowed to say that some things are wrong, such as homosexuality. I manage to get around that barrier to an extent by asking the students in my class to answer questions related to the subject. I also encourage them to inquire of their parents why homosexuality is wrong, along with the leaders in their church [or whatever house of worship they may attend].

MRS. FRANCES LEAF (high school psychologist): I work at a public high school, and the tolerance ideology is so readily accepted there. Our school has a Gay-Straight Alliance club on campus, and our school also observes the Day of Silence [a national youth movement that caters to lesbian, gay, bisexual, and transsexual people]. We had a legal case not long ago because a male student protested the Day of Silence by wearing a shirt with a Bible verse on it. The school made him take it off, so he filed a lawsuit. We also had a math teacher who had some messages about God in his classroom, such as "In God We Trust," and the district told him to take them down. That situation also turned into a lawsuit.

DUSTY SANDERSON (student, age 17): Most of the teachers at my school aren't Christians; they present a broad spectrum of beliefs and don't make a case for what's right or wrong. To deal with that as a Christian, I saturate myself with the Word of God so I'm less susceptible to outside forces that go against biblical truth.

BECCA YOUNKMAN (student, age 17): Sometimes I'll talk to my friends about something that's bothering me, such as abortion or homosexuality, and they'll make comments like, "Well, you're not being tolerant." One of my friends accused me of discriminating against gay people and judging them. I told her that I was only expressing my beliefs and that I don't hate gay people; I just hate their sin.

MR. AUSTIN SEFTON (youth leader): When I was in high school I was blessed to be in a church youth group that was Bible centered. Now that I'm a freshman in college, I'm starting to visit college Bible study groups, and I'm noticing that the tolerance mentality has seeped into the Christian culture. In one Christian club, somebody in the group said, "We need to invite more Hindus and Muslims to our sessions so we can hear what they have to say." Well, yes, we do want people of different religions to feel welcome at our Christian club, but we shouldn't allow them to preach their doctrines there. Buddhists and Hindus might be upstanding and moral people, but Christianity is more than just moralism—we're saved by grace and by the blood of Christ. ✿

What Say You?

1) Have you noticed the growing trend toward moral relativism (the denial of absolute truth) in our culture? How about at your school or among people you know?

2) As a Christian, how can you build an unshakable foundation of truth?

3) What would you say to a friend who believes that all religions and spiritual views are equal?

"Geeminelli!"

Check it out:

Proverbs 17:27

No, your eyes aren't deceiving you. The title of this chapter is really "Geeminelli!" (pronounced Jee-men-el-ee). Wanna know what it means? To be honest, I really don't know. All I can say with certainty is that it's my dad's favorite exclamatory word. Whenever he's baffled or overwhelmed by something, he proclaims "Geeminelli!" in a loud, drawn-out manner.

Then there's his second-most favorite: "Gadzooks!" This one actually was the title of a book that one of his employees wrote about my dad's leadership principles in the workplace. Don't ask me what *gadzooks* means either, because I haven't the foggiest. It's just a wacky expression I've heard my dad say ever since I was a kid—and sometimes loud enough that I could hear it at the other end of the house!

Finally, my dad utters one familiar slang word in moments of frustration (for example, when his beverage gets knocked over or his hotel key card won't open the door)—"Nuts!" I'll admit I've used "Nuts!" on occasion too, but thankfully I've never included the bizarre "Geeminelli!" or "Gadzooks!" in my vocabulary.

Now if I'm going to divulge my dad's slang list, it's only fair that I reveal my own frequently used favorites. Laugh if you want to, but these are my humdingers: "Crud!" and "Rats!" If I happen to chuck something into the garbage bin I didn't intend to or drip Coca-Cola on my shirt, it just feels good to grit my teeth and blurt out, "Rats!"

How about you? Do you have silly words you say in moments of anger or agitation? What are they? Hopefully they're rated G for "general audience." If they fall under a restricted category, then girlfriend, it's time to clean out those "files" and upgrade your vocabulary!

Have you considered that God is displeased with foul language? It's true. Check out these passages that are found in His Word:

"If anyone considers himself religious and yet does not keep a tight rein on his tongue, he deceives himself and his religion is worthless" (James 1:26).

"Nor should there be any obscenity, foolish talk or coarse joking, which are out of place, but rather thanksgiving" (Ephesians 5:4).

"May the words of my mouth and the meditation of my heart be pleasing in your sight, O LORD" (Psalm 19:14).

As you can see, the way you talk matters a great deal to the Lord. He wants you to be conscious about what you say and to glorify Him with your words.

That brings me to a very important point. As you know, some Christians say, "Oh my G--!" in casual conversation as if it's no big deal. Just last week I phoned a Christian woman about some gifts she wanted to donate to a ministry, and in her excitement she blurted out, "Oh my G--!" three times during our short conversation. I don't think she realized the seriousness of what she said.

The Bible is clear about the holiness of God. We are to stand in awe of Him and speak His name in reverence. "Our Father in heaven, hallowed [holy] be your name" (Matthew 6:9). As the third commandment warns, "You shall not misuse the name of the LORD your God, for the LORD will not hold anyone guiltless who misuses his name" (Exodus 20:7). The meaning of that Scripture is self-evident: unless you're talking to God or about Him, you shouldn't be using His name—certainly not as a "filler word" or as an emotional outburst. The same is true for Jesus Christ, the "Lord of lords and King of kings" (Revelation 17:14). His name is equally holy and should only be spoken in reverence.

As you know, there are other words that are not directly tied to God that are inappropriate for a Christian to say. A couple of months ago I was standing in line with my basket of canned cat food at a PetSmart store. I couldn't help but overhear two girls chatting in front of me, because one of them was very loud. She was also very attractive, and I noticed guys turning around to check her out and try to catch her eye. This girl seemed oblivious to their stares, though, because she was too busy giggling and gabbing with her friend. Then I heard her say the F word. Stock plummet! All of a sudden she didn't seem as pretty anymore. She was just another foulmouthed person who was imitating the patterns of the world.

As a Christian, you are called by God to be "set apart" (Psalm 4:3). That means the way you talk and act should be noticeably different from the rest of the world. I realize this can be a challenge in today's immoral climate. In addition to the foul language you probably hear on your school campus and in your neighborhood, you're also bombarded with profanity from the entertainment industry. Television, movies, music, and the Internet continue to push the envelope with greater perversion and obscenities. It's hard to be immune to their influence, even if you're using discretion in your choice of entertainment. That's why it's so important to make an unwavering decision to not use language that is dishonoring to the Lord.

Here's how one family dealt with this issue. My friend Kristin uses this simple sentence with her five kids whenever they heard a curse word on TV or in a movie: "We don't say that." Her kids (most of them teenagers) have heard that statement enough from their mom that now they say it themselves. If one of Kristin's daughters, for instance, hears a bad word in a DVD, she'll turn and look at her mom and say, "I know . . . 'we don't say that.'" It's just a little phrase, but it carries a big message.

If you've been guilty of using bad language lately, or even for an extended period of time, you can seek God's forgiveness and make a new start. I realize old habits can be hard to break, but Philippians 4:13 gives assurance that you "can do all things through Christ who strengthens [you]" (NKJV).

At my Bible study last year, one of the girls in our group (whom I'll refer to as Megan) shared that she had been struggling with using bad language. At the time, she was in the process of moving into a new home and was feeling stressed and disorganized. Megan admitted she had always had a problem with swearing, even as a Christian, but the pressure of relocating was making her less-than-clean vocabulary become more prevalent and unmanageable. Megan emphasized that because she wasn't raised in a Christian home, she heard her parents and siblings curse on a regular basis. She believed her flawed past was so embedded in her mind that she had no control over it. Her exact words were "I can't help it."

In a spirit of love, I reminded Megan that she could do all things through Christ. I also suggested our group pray together to petition God to enable her to overcome her addiction. We asked the Lord to break the ties that bound Megan and to help her achieve victory in that area of her life. Two weeks later when our group met again, Megan reported with a smile that she had become a lot more disciplined in her struggle with cursing. We rejoiced together and thanked God for His powerful work in Megan's life!

If the Lord can help Megan, He will surely do the same for you if you ask! The Bible teaches that "God is faithful; he will not let you be tempted beyond what you can bear. But when you are tempted, he will also provide a way out so that you can stand up under it" (1 Corinthians 10:13). That's a promise you can depend on! You don't ever have to feel overpowered by *any* form of sin, because God will give you the strength you need to resist it.

On a lighthearted note, may I encourage you to join my dad's and my "non–cuss word club"? You might not decide to add words like *geeminelli* or *nuts* into your vocabulary, but hopefully you'll come up with your own guiltfree exclamatories. Then, if the unfortunate moment comes when you squirt ketchup on your sleeve instead of your fries, you'll have the perfect word to fit the occasion!

"Do not let any unwholesome talk come out of your mouths, but only what is helpful for building others up according to their needs, that it may benefit those who listen" (Ephesians 4:29).

LET'S TALK ABOUT BAD LANGUAGE

ALYSON THOMAS (student, age 16): My close friends don't use bad language around me because they know I'll call them on it. The cheer squad that I'm involved with would be swearing a lot more if I wasn't in the group.

DAVID STRUM (student, age 15): Some of my friends at school refer to themselves as Christians, yet they talk like a bunch of sailors! I find that really sad and difficult to understand. They think they can't express themselves without adding expletives. I'll be walking through my school campus, and I'll pass a group of kids and hear a bunch of cuss words back-to-back—I mean, literally every other word! I'm tempted to carry a tape recorder around for just one day. Cussing at my school is like background noise, and some words are as common as the word *the*. The principal and teachers know it goes on, but they won't do anything to stop it. They talk about freedom of speech, and they say, "It's a free country." Fortunately, I don't hear kids using Jesus' name in vain very much. Most of them don't want to be associated with a specific "religion."

JENNA SALLADIN (student, age 17): Some of my friends from church who attend public school will occasionally slip and say a cuss word while they're at church. They'll say, "Whoops! I'm at church—I shouldn't have said that." What they're really saying is, "Oh, I'm with my Christian friends now, so I have to watch my mouth." They shouldn't be saying those words in any situation.

BEN TRAPP (student, age 15): Just about everybody has a foul mouth at my school—even the teachers cuss occasionally. I don't use bad language, but it's hard because I'm around it all the time. For example, I'm on the swim team, and if I'm upset about something, the other guys don't take me seriously because I don't cuss. It adds more pressure, and I feel like I'm not heard or acknowledged.

MR. WILLIAM ZUETEL (middle school teacher): You may think that the people around you haven't noticed that you're different from the rest of the crowd, but you'd be surprised. When I was a teen I went to Fort Knox for six weeks of Army training. Some of the guys noticed that I didn't cuss, and they teased me. I responded by telling them that I didn't need to do that. One day as I was stand-ing near my bunk, a group of guys came running toward me and asked, "Are you okay? What's wrong?" After assur-ing them that I was fine, one of them said, "We heard you cuss, and we know that you don't do that. We figured something really bad must have happened to you." As it turned out, it was someone else they had heard, and they mistook that person's voice for mine. I'll never forget the worried expressions on their faces, though. I hadn't com-prehended before that moment just how much they were observing my words and behavior.

JONATHAN YOUNKMAN (student, age 15): I have to won-der why people feel a need to cuss. Why is it so important? Does it make them feel cool?

ELISSA MASON (student, age 14): I attend public school, and I try to block out the profanity. I think bad language makes people look trashy in the way they present themselves. I have a good friend who attends my church and youth group, and she also attends my school. One day at school we were walking with some friends and she said a cuss word. It *really shocked me, and I lost some respect for her. She would never talk that way at church, but at school she thinks,* No one around here cares. *Well, God sees and cares, and so do I. It bothers me to see Christians who act one way on Sunday and another way on Monday. They're being hypocrites.*

JON SALLADIN *(student, age 15): I try to spend the majority of my time with people I want to emulate. That's how I stay away from bad language. But it's hard during football season when the guys let the curse words fly. I honestly don't know how they can string sentences together when every other word is profanity.*

MRS. MEGAN BARBER *(middle school teacher): I don't think students use bad language to show their emotions—they do it to fit in and be accepted. They observe people around them cussing, so why not? When students have cussed in my class, I make them call home and tell their parents exactly what they said. That tends to put a stop to it.*

MR. TIMOTHY STRANSKE *(high school teacher): Once a problem like foul language reaches a certain level, it's hard for a teacher to control it. I work at a public school, and if I were to send referrals for profanity, the administration would wonder why I was wasting my time. I can, however, control what is said within my classroom. If I hear a student say a cuss word, I make him or her come in for five or ten minutes during break or lunch. I tell that person that the word they used is inappropriate and will not be tolerated in my class. Quite often the student will be surprised and say, "What are you talking about? It's no big deal—I can talk that way in Mr. So-and-So's class." I tell them, "That doesn't matter. If you want to keep coming to my class,* you'll need to control your speech." I also remind the student that foul language isn't going to be accepted in a lot of other situations throughout his or her life.

PASTOR AUSTIN DUNCAN (youth minister): We're doing a series in our youth group entitled "The Sins of the Mouth" [based on James 3]. We covered the topic of gossiping one week, lying the second week, and now we're moving on to cussing. Part of maturity is not just keeping our speech clean but also using it to build people up and encourage them. A helpful acronym is THINK. Before speaking, ask yourself, Is it True? Is it Helpful? Is it Inspiring? Is it Necessary? Is it Kind? That's a good way to consider how our words need to glorify God. If we're rotten inside, then our speech will be rotten. It's a heart issue—a reflection of who you are in Christ.

If you heard a Christian friend say a cuss word, what would think of him or her?

BEN TRAPP (student, age 15): I'd be very surprised, and I'd question if he's a genuine Christian. I'd think he was a hypocrite, and I'd lose some respect for him.

JON SALLADIN (student, age 15): I'd be very disappointed, and I'd take my friend aside and tell him, "You're not setting a godly example." I'd also suggest that he repent.

What are some funny words you say in moments of anger, pain, or frustration?

DAVID STRUM (student, age 15): Chicken tenders!

JONATHAN YOUNKMAN (student, age 15): I like to say, "Cracker Jacks!" or, "Oh, Bessie!"

MIREN JOHNSEN (student, age 15): I don't say unique words, but my mom says, "Shin-diggies!" For instance, if she forgets to pick up my brother from his guitar lesson, she'll say, "Oh, shin-diggies! I forgot!"

JON SALLADIN (student, age 15): I know it's a mouth-ful, but sometimes when I'm mad, I'll say, "Shredded beef tacos!" I'll also say, "Oh, snap!" or "Bummer." My mom says, "Shoot" all the time, and for a while she got into a habit of saying, "Shoot a pickle!" One day I got so sick of hearing it that I took a pickle, shot it in the backyard with my BB gun, and handed it to her. ✿

What Say You?

1) As a Christian, why is it important for you to avoid "unwholesome talk" (Ephesians 4:29)?

2) How do you feel when you hear someone using God's name or Jesus' name in a disrespectful way?

3) What decision(s) have you made about using language that dishonors the Lord?

4) How can your choice of words be a witness to others?

Family Matters

Check it out:

Matthew 5:9

Did you ever get a spanking when you were a kid? Perhaps more than one? My mom and dad certainly did not "spare the rod" from my backside. In fact, my dad wrote a few best-selling books for parents on that subject, such as *Dare to Discipline*, *The Strong-Willed Child*, and *Parenting Isn't for Cowards*. Believe me when I say that my dad was no coward! He made sure my defiance was met with some good old-fashioned discipline. I can remember one incident, which I call "the grand finale," as though it were yesterday.

The school I attended was participating in a private party for schools in the area at Knott's Berry Farm (a popular amusement park in Southern California). Anyone who is well acquainted with me knows that I love amusement parks! As a kid I used to get so excited the night before going to Disneyland that I found it difficult to fall asleep. I still get hyped before going there—what is called "the happiest place on earth"—the only difference is that now the thought of the Pirates of the Caribbean ride doesn't cause me to stare at the ceiling in anticipation.

On that particular day, my sights were set on Knott's Berry Farm, and I was thrilled to be going with some good friends from school—Erin, Deanna, Mitzi, and Lisa. Erin's mother provided transportation, and as we cruised down the highway we were full of pent-up energy. We couldn't wait to cut loose in the giant playground and do whatever we wanted until the park closed at midnight. That was the plan, or so we thought, until Erin's mom dropped the bomb. Shortly before we arrived at Knott's Berry Farm she told us that she had something going on that night and would need to pick us up at 4 p.m. *What!* It was already noon, and we weren't even at the entrance gate yet! My three friends and I explained to her that we had informed our parents that we would be staying until midnight, but she wasn't open to negotiation.

I pretended to be okay with the four o'clock arrangement, but as I said good-bye to Erin's mom in the parking lot, I knew I had a mission: I would find a way for us to stay at Knott's Berry Farm until closing time as we had originally planned. We were *not* going home in the afternoon while the other kids at the park partied until the clock struck twelve. Our day of thrills would not be squelched just because Erin's mom had some lousy "previous engagement."

For the next few hours, we ran from one attraction to the next and ate pizza and ice cream, but as it got closer to four o'clock, I knew it was time to deal with the dilemma. I had a brief huddle with Mitzi, Lisa, and Deanna, and we agreed unanimously that we weren't ready to call it a day. Mitzi solved the problem by offering to phone her mom later and arrange transportation. Good strategy! Now we had to take care of one more detail. As Erin prepared to leave, we informed her of our decision and asked her to tell her mom that we would be going home with Mitzi's mother instead. Erin seemed a little disturbed with the change in itinerary, but she agreed and left.

We should have smelled trouble when Erin came back to the park to look for us. She found us in the Log Ride line and reported that her mom wanted us to come to the car immediately so she could take us home. Nope—we had made our decision. We weren't budging. Once again, we asked Erin to tell her mother that we would be fine and to go on without us. If I had been older and wiser, I might have understood the responsibility Erin's mom felt to return us safely to our parents. But my only concern that day was getting what I wanted.

For the rest of the evening, my three friends and I enjoyed countless rides, giggled, and consumed all the french fries, soda pop, and cotton candy we could handle. Around 11 p.m. we headed to a public telephone (no cell phones back then) so Mitzi could call her mom and arrange for her to pick us up. Things spiraled down from there. While Mitzi was on the phone with her mother, I could tell by the worried expression on her face and the muffled words coming through the line that we were in deep water. Mitzi hung up the phone and gave me the bad news: Erin's mom was very upset and had called all our parents. Busted!

Mitzi's mom was furious. She ordered her daughter to have us wait in the guest relations center until she could get to the amusement park. After an agonizing hour, both of Mitzi's parents arrived to pick us up. We received quite a lecture from her mother, who couldn't believe we would be so irresponsible as well as disrespectful to Erin's mom. As I sat there listening to her rant and rave, I began to dread going home. I knew my parents would not be waiting for me with a hug and a "Hope you had a nice time."

It was a correct assumption. My dad was not a happy camper, and he implemented the advice he had given to thousands of other parents whose kids were defiant. It was a tough evening, to be sure.

The next day at school Deanna confessed that she, too, had received a spanking when she got home. Misery loves company.

That was the last spanking I ever received. As I got older, Mom and Dad began using more creative methods for punishment, such as grounding me from the use of my stereo, making me write sentences fifty to one hundred times ("I will not bug Ryan; I will not bug Ryan . . ."), and even taking my bedroom door off its hinges for a period of time. Talk about a breach of privacy!

For the most part, though, my adolescent years were tranquil at home. There was a lot of love, laughter, and good times. Whenever I did clash with my parents, the conflicts usually involved one of three issues: broken curfews, tardiness to school or church, and money matters. Those were "the biggies."

What are the hot buttons with your parents? Are your disagreements with them related to the long hours you spend on your cell phone, the mess you leave in the bathroom before going to school, or cranking up your music too loud? Do sparks fly over the amount of junk food you eat, the way you style your hair, or your clothing selections? As one twelve-year-old girl said, quoting her mother's distaste for her shoes, "You ain't wearin' them things!"

Would you believe me if I told you that it's *normal* to

experience conflicts with our parents? It has to do with our ambition for power and independence. We all want to make our own decisions and run our own lives—that desire lies deep within the human spirit. Even toddlers challenge the authority of their parents early on.

The Knott's Berry Farm incident is a good example of my own cry for autonomy. I desperately wanted to be my own boss, and for a few hours at least I managed to succeed, although not without infuriating five sets of parents and subjecting my backside to jeopardy.

Human beings, both children and adults, are imperfect creatures. King David wrote about himself, "Surely I was sinful at birth, sinful from the time my mother conceived me" (Psalm 51:5). This is true of us all; our inclination to do wrong was inherited from Adam and Eve. That automatic tendency to sin is also why we must have a perfect Savior, Jesus Christ, to forgive our sins and make us a "new creation" (2 Corinthians 5:17). Even then, Satan tries to get us to do what we know is wrong, especially in our relationships with others.

The apostle Paul wrote a wonderful recipe for having peace in a family. We find it in Colossians 3:12-14: "As God's chosen people, holy and dearly loved, clothe yourselves with compassion, kindness, humility, gentleness and patience. Bear with each other and forgive whatever grievances you may have against one another. Forgive as the Lord forgave you. And over all these virtues put on love, which binds them all together in perfect unity."

I know it's easier to read those words than to put them into action, so I've developed a few strategies for displaying kindness and compassion toward your parents during times of conflict. Try this:

1. Ask your mom or dad if you can set up a time to sit down and discuss the dilemma together in a calm manner.

2. Instead of lashing out in anger, head to your room, close the door (gently), and talk to the Lord about the situation. Prayerfully petition Him to grant you wisdom in communicating with your parents and to bring resolution to the problem.

3. If you've tried to respectfully negotiate with your parents and they still say no to your wishes, then accept their authority and put the matter to rest. Don't fuss and fume because you didn't get what you wanted. No conflict is worth creating bitter memories that will linger into your adult life. You don't want to have regrets over things you said and did while growing up.

Did you know that eight times in Scripture (two times in the Old Testament and six in the New Testament), children are told to honor their parents?[1] It's one of the Ten Commandments (see Exodus 20:12) and is followed with a promise: "That you may live long in the land."

May I urge you to be a peacemaker in your family—not just when it comes to your parents, but with your brothers and sisters, too? If that isn't one of your strengths, ask the Lord to help you, and He will. "The wisdom that comes from heaven is first of all pure; then peace-loving, considerate, submissive, full of mercy and good fruit, impartial and sincere. Peacemakers who sow in peace raise a harvest of righteousness" (James 3:17-18).

---

[1] Exodus 20:12; Deuteronomy 5:16; Matthew 15:4, 19:19; Mark 7:10, 10:19; Luke 18:20; Ephesians 6:2.

Here's my prayer for each of us: "Father, give us the grace to care more about creating harmony in our families than getting our own way, and help us to display a Christlike attitude in times of disagreement. In Jesus' name, Amen."

LET'S TALK ABOUT FAMILIES

JULIA SALLADIN (student, age 18): My parents trust me, but that doesn't mean they're going to withdraw their opinions, and I wouldn't want them to. Even after I graduate from college, I'm still going to seek their advice and counsel. I'm learning as I go, but my parents have already been down some of the paths I'm walking. They're wiser because they've lived longer.

MRS. MEGAN BARBER *(middle school teacher): The most successful parent-child relationships I've seen are the ones where both parties work together to come to solutions. You have to be willing to do this, however. It's similar to being a child of God. Instead of resisting who He is and what He desires for our lives, we need to work with Him to accomplish something.*

MRS. FRANCES LEAF *(high school psychologist): A lot of students complain that their parents don't understand them. (I think I said the same thing to my mom and dad a few times as I was growing up.) Often, both parents work, so the kids end up turning to friends for support instead of their families. I also see a lot of kids whose parents are divorced, so the kids divide their time between the two, which causes a great deal of stress. Another problem is related to unrealistic expectations that some parents have in regard to academic achievement. Because college* admission is very competitive these days, some parents put a lot of pressure on their kids to achieve, achieve, achieve. Not that this is wrong, but it's not uncommon for me to see students who are stressed out because they're taking several AP courses, doing volunteer work, studying for SATs, and trying to start a new club at school.

Describe an area of weakness between you and your parents and how you're working on it.

FRANKIE OGAZ (student, age 16): I have to confess that I get into a lot of arguments with my parents. I'm not good at hiding my feelings, so if I'm upset about something, I'll say it. But lately when my mom and I get into arguments, I've been trying to remain calm. I know that the minute I raise my voice she won't take me seriously, but if I explain my feelings in a respectful way, she listens more. I've realized that God put my parents in a position of authority over me for a good reason, so I have to accept their decisions. Sometimes it helps to try to look at a situation from their point of view.

DAVID STRUM (student, age 15): My mom works me over for not practicing my voice lessons enough, so I'm trying to be better about that. I'm also learning that when she asks me to clean something, she means now! I used to think "now" meant "later," but that didn't work out too good.

ALYSON THOMAS (student, age 16): God knew that kids would not want to obey their parents, so He gave us the command, "Honor your father and mother." When I'm involved in a conflict with my parents, I'm not thinking, Oh, this is what's best for me or My parents love me so much. *No, all I'm thinking about at the time is,* I want to be right. *I can show respect for my parents by shutting up sometimes. That's the best way to respond when I'm angry because the moment I open my mouth, destructive words come out. It's better to control my tongue.*

BEN TRAPP *(student, age 15): My mom can get real "naggy," which annoys me. But I'm trying to show more respect for her as my authority figure.*

REBECCA YOUNG *(student, age 16): Sometimes my mom and I go shopping and have a great time; then later we get into a fight, and I feel horrible. I know I need to respect my mom, but it's hard to control my words when I'm angry. Lately I've been trying to exercise self-control by walking away when I feel like saying something harsh. I need to pray about that more often and ask God to help me.*

SARAH UTTERBACK *(student, age 16): I rarely argue with my mom—we have a great relationship—but my dad and I get into fights. Sometimes I think he can't relate to me and what it's like to be in high school, but times haven't changed that much since he was a teenager. I know that he had to deal with a lot of the same issues, so I've been trying to be conscious of that.*

SAMANTHA BOWSER *(student, age 17): I get into stupid arguments with my mom because we're both stubborn and want our own way. Sometimes when my mom is saying something I disagree with, I keep my comments to myself. Then when she walks away, I'll go into my bedroom, close the door, and let it all out. I've only done this a couple of times, but it really helps.*

MR. AUSTIN SEFTON *(youth leader): It's really important to be on the same level as your parents. If you're doing something against their wishes, such as spending time with a guy they don't approve of, then you're not in God's will. He makes it clear that you need to "honor your father and mother." It doesn't matter if you think it's okay to do something. If you don't have your parents' consent, then you're in sin. I have my own issues to work on. Sometimes my temper flares, and I talk back to my mom. How am I going to resolve that? Only by spending time with Jesus—by reading His Word and asking Him to help me.*

Describe an area of weakness between you and your siblings and how you're working on it.

BEN TRAPP *(student, age 15): I'm really good with computers, but my brother is computer illiterate. He'll ask me questions like, "How do you get the printer to work?" So I'll take a look and discover the printer wasn't turned on or plugged in. That's annoying, especially when I'm tired and I've dragged myself off the sofa to help. Also, my sister will take things out of my room without asking, like my camera, for example, and then act totally innocent. She'll fake tears, and my mom will get mad at me. My mom will say, "You're older, and it's your responsibility . . ." That's another source of frustration for me. But I'm trying to be less bossy and more patient.*

ELISSA MASON *(student, age 14): My brother and I have a great relationship, but sometimes we become self-centered and snap at each other. That's something we've been trying to work on.*

BECCA YOUNKMAN (student, age 17): I have three broth-ers, and we don't have a close relationship. We don't hug each other and say, "I love you." For the past year, though, we've been spending more time together and becoming more open. One of my brothers has taken me on long-distance drives to different locations, and we've shared some good conversations in the car.

JONATHAN YOUNKMAN (student, age 15): I used to get angry at my brothers when they would make jokes and goof around. I now find it very effective to just go into my bedroom and close the door.

JON SALLADIN (student, age 15): I have four sisters, and I like to be the leader, but so does my older sister Julia. She and I clash on occasion, but I know I should let her lead because she's older. I also have a tendency to get mad over stupid things and storm out, so I'm trying to become more patient. Another thing I'm working on is letting my parents do the parenting with my younger siblings.

JENNA SALLADIN (student, age 17): Because I have a large family, there's never a time when everybody's out of the house and I can be by myself. I like to have quiet time, so I get annoyed with the constant noise. When I do sit down to spend some time by myself, my younger siblings are always needing help with something. I try to remember that they don't realize that I need time to be by myself, so when they ask me to do something, I say, "Okay, I'll come help you in a minute, but right now I need to be alone." ❁

What Say You?

1) Name a time when you experienced conflict with your mom or dad. What did you learn from that disagreement?

2) Think of an ongoing area of conflict between you and your parents. How might you improve it?

3) How does God want you to respond to your parents in moments of conflict?

4) Think of something kind to do this week to demonstrate your love for your parents.

Good Company

Check it out:

Psalm 101:3-4

One day I was chatting with a Starbucks employee named Josh while I waited for him to prepare my grande-size, nonfat, no-whip mocha latte. He was telling me that just a few days earlier, he and a friend had found a wallet with credit cards in it. His friend suggested that they go across the street and use the cards to make purchases, but Josh was adamantly opposed. He wasted no time hopping in his car and driving off. He told me the reason he didn't stick around was because he had definite goals for his future and didn't want to mess them up. As he put it, "I want to stay clean." I complimented Josh on his wise decision and agreed that he'd done the right thing. "Good for you!" I said.

I don't know if Josh is a Christian, but his response to his friend's immoral suggestion falls in line with 1 Timothy 6:10-11: "The love of money is a root of all kinds of evil. Some people, eager for money, have wandered from the faith and pierced themselves with many griefs. But you, man of God, flee from all this, and pursue righteousness, godliness, faith, love, endurance and gentleness."

Even though he may not have known this verse, Josh fled from evil, while his friend was willing to do something that eventually would pierce him with grief.

After I left Starbucks and headed to my car, I thought about my own close friends and their character. I couldn't imagine any of them using stolen credit cards! The mere thought was totally absurd. It's not just because my friends are considerate, law-abiding citizens. The main reason they would never steal someone's money is because they're followers of Christ. The Holy Spirit dwells within them (see 2 Timothy 1:14); therefore, they have convictions about not doing things that contradict biblical principles.

Although I've lost touch with some people through the years and have formed new relationships, one thing has stayed consistent from my childhood until today: my closest friends have always been Christians. Even when I attended a public high school, some of my friends from church who went to the same school were the ones I hung out with during lunch and did activities with on the weekends.

Now, I'll be completely honest with you. If you think my friends and I spent the majority of our time keeping our hands folded in our laps, singing hymns, and quoting Christian authors like C. S. Lewis, think again! We were typical teenagers. Sometimes we got a little carried away—cracking jokes and playing pranks. One night a friend took all the leaves he'd raked from his yard and piled them by our front door. You can imagine my mom's surprise when she opened the door and an avalanche of leaves spilled into the entryway. Guess who cleaned it up? The next day at the crack of dawn, my friend Kristin and I transported two garbage bags of leaves to that same guy's house and scattered them all over his yard. Then we jumped into our car and sped off, giggling all the way home. Ah, sweet revenge!

Even though my friends and I did some wacky things, it was all in good fun, and we resisted the pressure to drink, do drugs, and be sexually active. Our church youth group provided a safe environment where we didn't have to worry about wild parties and other worldly activities going on around us. We had an awesome pastor—very cool and outgoing—who made Sunday school relevant to our lives and worth attending. In fact, a couple of guys liked it so much they drove two hours to get there every Sunday.

In the summertime, our group had beach BBQs, choir tours, weekend getaways, and mission trips. There was always something going on. A favorite activity of mine was our Sunday night "Triple Fs" (fun, food, and fellowship) that occurred once a month throughout the year. I even hosted a couple of them, which was an ideal arrangement for me because my parents paid for the pizza and snacks.

High school can be a tough experience, with lots of pressures to conform and fit in, but thanks in part to my church youth group, my high school years were happy ones. How about you? Are you involved in some type of Christian fellowship? Is there a youth ministry at your church or school that you're part of? If not, I highly recommend you make a few calls to find one. Ask your friends and pray for guidance. I'm sure the Lord will help you discover a vibrant mix of Christians to socialize with. You might also consider getting involved in Student Venture, which is a Christian outreach for teens that is affiliated with Campus Crusade for Christ (a ministry to students at colleges and universities). To see if there's a Student Venture ministry at your high school or to obtain information, go to http://www.studentventure.com or http://www.ccci.org. If your school doesn't have a Student Venture group, think about starting one! Just click the "Coaching Center" link on the Student Venture Web site for more information.

With all the pressures out there, it's essential that you develop friendships with people who share your faith. I often think of 1 Corinthians 15:33, which says, "Bad company corrupts good character." It would be difficult for *anybody* to stay strong in the Lord while hanging around friends who party, swear, and sleep around. I know some Christians who have joined in their friends' bad behavior and "gone off the deep end" as a result of doing that very thing. They got involved with the wrong crowd, and soon they were partying too. Some of them really messed up their lives! I'm thinking of one guy in particular who started frequenting clubs with non-Christians and ended up having a baby with his girlfriend and becoming an alcoholic from his heavy partying and drinking. He now attends AA (Alcoholics Anonymous) meetings to combat his addiction.

Linking up with other believers is important, not only to keep yourself accountable and pure, but also for developing lasting friendships. Some of the people I keep in touch with today are friends I met in my church's high school group. I even have a few whom I met in Sunday school when I was a kid! They are lifelong friends who share my values and convictions.

I pray you'll experience that blessing too. Why not make an effort right now to surround yourself with Christian friends? I'm not talking about the kind of people who label themselves Christians but then live by the world's standards. I'm referring to friends who are committed to growing in their relationship with the Lord; people who are sold out for Him 100 percent! People just like *you.*

"Blessed is the man who does not walk in the counsel of the wicked or stand in the way of sinners or sit in the seat of mockers. But his delight is in the law of the LORD, and on his law he meditates day and night" (Psalm 1:1-2).

LET'S TALK ABOUT FRIENDS

JON SALLADIN (student, age 15): You turn into the people you hang with. That's why I try to surround myself with Christian friends. I can be myself around them—they love and accept me, and they'll forgive me when I make a confession. The guys on my league football team aren't Christians, so I don't feel as comfortable around them.

DAVID STRUM (student, age 15): If we have the wrong friends, they will take us down! It's like having one good dog and one bad dog. If you feed the bad dog more than the good dog, the bad dog will grow stronger and overpower the good dog. The same is true the other way around. We need to be feeding our minds with the right stuff and hanging around solid, Christian friends.

ERIN DIEFENBACH (student, age 17): I've been involved in secular choirs my entire life. Last year I tried out for the top choir at my school and got accepted. I was so excited, but then I began to wonder if God wanted me to be in that particular choir. I wrestled with the decision for quite a while and then decided to call my pastor. He said that he thought God had already given me the answer but I was resisting. At that point I started to cry, and I knew I had to quit the school choir. It turned out to be the right decision because most of the people in the group were worldly and into themselves, and I felt negative when I was around them. In addition to that, the choir director was a jerk, and he would scream and cuss. I realized that God didn't want me spending so much time with those people just for the purpose of being onstage and performing. What has resulted from my decision is that whenever someone asks me why I quit the choir, I have an opportunity to take a stand for what I believe.

BECCA YOUNKMAN (student, age 17): Having attended public school in the past and now being homeschooled, I have two sets of friends—both Christians and not. Recently one of my non-Christian friends from public school had a birthday party, and even though her parents were there, the atmosphere felt ungodly. I felt weird and uncomfortable. It made me realize how much I enjoy being around Christian friends. I don't have to wonder if they're questioning whether something is moral or not, because we're all in agreement. While I was attending public school, my friends knew I was a Christian, but they didn't always take that into consideration when they were making sexual innuendos and crude jokes.

DUSTY SANDERSON (student, age 17): I was homeschooled until high school, and now that I'm attending a public school, I've noticed that being around non-Christians really brings me down. It's easy for me to pick up their words, attitudes, and mannerisms. All that negativity rubs off on me, which is something I didn't realize before I started attending public school. People can corrupt each other—it's like spreading toxic waste around, and everybody gets infected. There's verbal tearing down that goes on and not much respect for teachers. I'm on the baseball team, and instead of my teammates working together for a common goal, everybody is out for themselves; plus there are little cliques within the team. I don't get a lot of support. That's why my church youth group is so great. It's much more uplifting to be around Christian friends who share my values and beliefs.

MR. MATT NORTHRUP *(high school dean): I highly recommend that young ladies build strong friendships with godly people within their church and youth group. I also suggest that they actively seek out an older woman to mentor them—someone to help them make wise decisions as they navigate through the sometimes rough waters of adolescence. A lot of older women don't understand how much they can give, and they're not aware that the younger generation is looking for answers and guidance. That's why I recommend that a teen girl seek out someone after asking God to help her unite with the right person.*

MR. AUSTIN SEFTON *(youth leader): Proverbs 27:17 says, "As iron sharpens iron, so one man sharpens another." When you have solid Christian friends and you're encouraging each other in the Word, confessing things to one another, and perhaps confronting each other if one of you is failing in some way, it helps all of you to grow spiritually. Even if you have only one or two solid Christian friends, stick with them and grow together.*

What are your thoughts about peer pressure?

ALYSON THOMAS *(student, age 16): As Christians we're supposed to stand out and not fit in with the crowd. Some of my friends think I'm a "goody two-shoes," but I really don't care. I'm fine with that. I also think it's important to* keep each other accountable. For example, one of my girl-friends could easily succumb to the party scene—she has a lot of opportunities—but she knows that I would get on her case if she pursued it.

MR. WILLIAM ZUETEL (middle school teacher): In middle school and high school there's an incredible amount of pressure to fit in, and a risk of being made fun of if you don't. But remember that the kids at your school who are so important to you right now will scatter to the four winds after high school graduation.

REBECCA YOUNG (student, age 16): There are kids in my math class who drink and smoke pot on the weekends, and I think to myself, If they're doing that now, what are they going to be doing when they're twenty-one? They're prob-ably going to be into harder drugs and will be a lot more messed up. I don't want to have anything to do with that lifestyle. I'm only interested in forming friendships with Christians who share my values.

SARAH UTTERBACK (student, age 16): It's a good idea to make a commitment to yourself and to God about the things that are off-limits for you. For myself, I made some decisions a long time ago, and I've stayed with them.

ERIN DIEFENBACH (student, age 17): When we think of peer pressure, we often relate it to cigarettes, drugs, and alcohol, but gossiping is a big issue too. A lot of female conversations center on gossip, and I feel uncomfortable when I hear friends throwing jabs about each other. Sometimes I'll just walk away. I've been criticized with comments like, "Oh, you think you're too good for this conversation."

SAMANTHA BOWSER (student, age 17): I'm a person who can be easily persuaded to do something—like gossiping, for example. That's why it's important for me to have an accountability partner. When I'm with a group of people, I need at least one good friend there who will help me to make wise decisions. As for gossiping, my mom has always said that if you gossip about someone, it gives a message to the person you're talking to that you would gossip about him or her, too. I always think of that when I'm talking with someone.

MR. TIMOTHY STRANSKE (high school teacher): As far as peer pressure is concerned, some things are headed in the right direction, such as avoiding cigarettes. Thanks to the advertising campaign against smoking, teens are accepting the idea that smoking is gross, so it's becoming less popular. There are some instances where peer pressure can actually yield positive results.

MRS. MEGAN BARBER (middle school teacher): Everyone has a need to feel special and valued. At the school where I teach, the students try to accomplish that for themselves by finding a group they can fit into. They wear the same clothes and shoes as their friends in an effort to feel accepted and cherished. Other students act out by being nonconformists, but they're really seeking attention too. They just go about it in a different way. All of this behavior is rooted in the need to feel special.

What are some activities you enjoy doing with your friends?

JONATHAN YOUNKMAN (student, age 15): My friends and I like to hang at the food court at the mall—we get ice cream and go to popular places like Starbucks. We also enjoy all-night movie nights at someone's house.

JENNA SALLADIN (student, age 17): I enjoy spending an evening with my friends, painting fingernails and giving each other facials.

DAVID STRUM (student, age 15): I like paintball or airsofting, which is similar to paintball, except we shoot a small plastic ball. These games aren't just for guys—the girls get into them too, and they have a great time.

ELISSA MASON (student, age 14): I like getting a group together to play hide-and-seek at night. I also enjoy cosmic bowling, which is like regular bowling except the balls and pins glow in the dark.

MARIN JOHNSEN (student, age 15): I really don't enjoy hanging out in large groups because some kind of drama always occurs. But I love having sleepovers with my friends, with nail polish and movies. Whenever my dad goes hunting with my friend's dad, we get together with our moms and sisters to eat goodies and watch Jane Austen movies.

MATT GODSHALL (student, age 14): My friends associate my home with cookies because we always end up baking cookies when they come over. I don't have the skills to start from scratch, so Toll House is where it's at!

JON SALLADIN (student, age 15): My friends and I love to play hide-and-seek at department stores. We hide in the garden area, the dressing rooms, or the bicycle area. One time my friend jumped over me and we got in trouble, so now we take the energy level down a notch.

BEN TRAPP (student, age 15): At my church we have what is called the Mud Bowl, which is a big pit of mud. We play a lot of games like tug-of-war, and the girls totally get into it. In fact, I think the girls are more into it than the guys! I've invited some non-Christian friends to the Mud Bowl because it's a great way to get them to come to a church event.

BECCA YOUNKMAN (student, age 17): After my brother's basketball games, we go out to eat with friends and family members and have a great time.

DUSTY SANDERSON (student, age 17): I enjoy going somewhere with my friends where we can hang out and talk, such as a restaurant or a bowling alley. I like to play laser tag too.

MR. AUSTIN SEFTON (youth leader): When I was in high school, my church youth group used to go to the local homeless shelter and help those who were in need. Not only were we reaching out to homeless people with food and spiritual restoration, we were also building Christian friendships within our group. It's difficult for a group to fall into sin when they're doing things to further the Kingdom of God.

PASTOR AUSTIN DUNCAN (youth minister): Teens are experts at having fun—they can have a good time just about anywhere, even in a field of grass! In our youth group we do activities such as broomball, but we also do outreach events, such as visiting hospitals and ministering to the patients there. ❀

What Say You?

1) Do you know a Christian friend who has suffered in his or her relationship with the Lord as a result of hanging around nonbelievers? Think of one way you can be an example to that person. Pray for him or her.

2) Why is it important to surround yourself with friends who love God and are committed to growing in their faith?

3) Name a Christian you'd like to get to know better. What qualities do you admire in that person?

Salt and Light

Check it out:

Ephesians 5:8-9

Shelly didn't smile much. A divorced mother of one grown son, her life consisted of working two jobs, smoking cigarettes, and watching soap operas that she recorded on her VCR. A menial existence, to be sure.

I became acquainted with Shelly when someone recommended her as a manicurist. I started having her do my fingernails twice a month at the salon where she worked, and during that time we discussed many subjects, including Christianity.

Shelly was not a Christian. She believed that people of faith used their relationship with God as a crutch because they weren't strong enough to deal with their difficulties on their own. From her perspective, praying about one's problems was nothing more than a sign of weakness. I explained to Shelly that my relationship with the Lord defines who I am, and He is everything to me—not a crutch to lean on. Shelly wasn't convinced. I knew it was futile to try to convince her otherwise, so I continued to pray for her, and I looked for opportunities to plant seeds of truth in our conversations.

One afternoon while Shelly was buffing my fingernails, she casually mentioned that a friend had taken her to a local "harvest festival" (an evangelistic outreach event). She told me that at the end of the festival, a crowd of people had streamed to the front of the stadium to accept Christ.

"Why didn't you go too?" I asked.

Shelly didn't make eye contact as she continued buffing my fingernails under the lamp.

"I wasn't ready," she answered.

At that moment I knew there was hope! The fact that Shelly had said, "I wasn't ready," rather than "I didn't want to" or "I wasn't interested," told me that she might be open to receiving Christ at a later time. I prayed for her more diligently and even placed her name at the front of a church sanctuary one Sunday when a pastor asked for written prayer requests. I knew that the Lord had put Shelly on my heart, and I was determined to do my part to win her for Jesus!

I eventually stopped getting my fingernails professionally manicured, but I made an effort to stay in touch with Shelly. Two years passed, and right before her sixtieth birthday, the Lord seemed to say to me, "It's time."

When I called Shelly on her special day, she told me that she had received my birthday card and appreciated that I had remembered. We shared a lighthearted conversation about a variety of topics, and then I began to wade into matters of greater importance. I used her celebration of a milestone as an opportunity to talk about life and eternity.

After sharing my testimony, I asked Shelly a significant question: "If you were to die tonight and stand before God, and He were to ask you, 'Shelly, why should I let you into my heaven?' what would you say?"

"I'd tell God that I tried to be a good person," Shelly replied.

"That's a logical answer," I said, but then I told Shelly that "being good" isn't enough—God expects us to be perfect (see Matthew 5:48). Even one sinful thought or deed makes us unworthy to enter His Kingdom. Our sin separates us from God but I explained that Jesus bridged the gap of separation for us by dying on the cross for our sins. He purchased a place in heaven for us by His sacrifice, and all we need to do to have eternal life is to accept that free gift from Him. At that point I asked Shelly if she would like to receive the gift of eternal life by accepting Jesus into her heart. I could barely contain my tears and excitement when she replied, "Yes!" At my suggestion, she repeated every word I prayed and asked Jesus to forgive her sins and come into her heart. It was a defining moment for her, and amazingly it happened right at the beginning of a new birthday year.

Regarding my role in that scenario, I can tell you that leading Shelly to Christ was nothing short of exhilarating! To know that I played a part in rescuing a lost soul was more rewarding than winning the Nobel Prize or an Oscar or a Grammy. Those awards will eventually tarnish and be destroyed, but the reward of knowing that a person you led to Christ is bound for heaven will last forever. In addition to that blessing, God has promised to reward us someday for the work that we accomplished for Him. "Whatever you do, work at it with all your heart, as working for the Lord, not for men, since you know that you will receive an inheritance from the Lord as a reward" (Colossians 3:23-24).

Given all that motivation, what is it about the prospect of sharing our faith that causes most of us to tense up? With the Lord's help, I was able to witness to Shelly, but truth be told, I have never been at ease when talking to nonbelievers about Jesus. It's not my greatest spiritual gift. Perhaps the main reason I'm uncomfortable is that I've never been good at dealing with rejection, even if it's not personal.

For example, I once invited a friend of a friend to lunch, knowing that she was an atheist and a New Age devotee. I was hoping that I might have an opportunity to make inroads with her on a spiritual level. When our meals arrived, I asked her if I could pray before we ate, and she flippantly replied, "You can pray on your own if you want—I don't really pray." That comment felt like a slap in my face, even though it wasn't necessarily a personal assault. Nevertheless, it stung. I felt rather foolish as I bowed my head to silently thank God for my meal while the person sitting next to me was already chomping away.

Yes, rejection *does* come as a result of sharing our Christian faith at times. If you're unsure, just read about Jesus' experiences in the New Testament, as well as the experiences of His disciples and the apostle Paul, among others. They were rejected to the point of being beaten, thrown in prison, and even killed. Even today, Christians continue to be mistreated in countries such as Sudan and China. Some Christians are tortured and killed just for having prayer gatherings in their homes with fellow believers. Fortunately for us as Americans living in the twenty-first century, the odds of that happening as a result of our devotion to Christ are slim (at least for this moment in time). We have the freedom to talk about Jesus without fearing for our lives. So why is it difficult to do?

If the notion of sharing your faith with someone causes you to get the jitters, ask the Lord to help you gain courage and confidence. You might also try the approach I used with

Shelly by giving your own testimony—relaying what God did to bring you to faith in Christ and how you've grown in your relationship with Him. That's always a good place to start. Remember that whenever you witness to someone, it's never a two-way conversation—it's a *three-way* conversation between you, the other person, and the Holy Spirit. The Spirit has the responsibility to convict and change a person's heart, so while you're talking to someone about Jesus or sharing a Bible verse, the Spirit is speaking to that individual as well.

Jesus called us to be "the light of the world" (Matthew 5:14). Imagine standing in the desert on a dark, moonless night, gazing at a lighted city on a hill. Wouldn't it sparkle and shine like a precious gemstone? That's what Jesus meant when He gave the instruction to "let your light shine before men, that they may see your good deeds and praise your Father in heaven" (Matthew 5:16).

He also taught us to be "the salt of the earth" (Matthew 5:13). I don't know about you, but I love those flavorful granules on my fries and chips (and just about everything else)! Food is pretty bland without salt. From a spiritual perspective, we need to retain our saltiness. In other words, our behavior is to be distinctly different from those who are living by the world's standards. Ever heard the old saying, "He's not worth his salt"? As followers of Christ, if we're not representing Him well in the things that we say and do, then we're not worth our salt either. Jesus made a powerful statement in Matthew 5:13: "If the salt loses its saltiness, how can it be made salty again? It is no longer good for anything, except to be thrown out and trampled by men."

Salt is a preservative—it stings, it heals, it seasons, it

helps things to grow. We should be having that effect on those around us by our example and by sharing our faith.

Is your light burning brightly enough for people to notice? What "good works" do they see you doing that distinguish you from nonbelievers? Set an example for them by keeping your spiritual sodium level high and your light glowing at the highest wattage. That's the way to reflect positively upon your heavenly Father.

LET'S TALK ABOUT WITNESSING

ELISSA MASON (student, age 14): Recently I attended Dare to Share, an amazing conference about the need to share your Christian faith. One thing the speakers emphasized was the importance of memorizing Scripture, because if you don't know Scripture, how can you live it out? That really hit me, so I've challenged myself to memorize one verse each week. I want to become more familiar with God's Word.

PASTOR AUSTIN DUNCAN (youth minister): Christian teens who attend public school go into a mission field five days a week. They have so many opportunities to be effective witnesses for Christ. One guy from our church youth group started a Bible club at his school. It's a small group—about thirty-plus kids—but the club is a witness for Christ in a totally Christless place. We are Jesus' ambassadors, and He is spreading the message of salvation through us. If we're going to be effective witnesses for Him, we have to have a clear understanding of the gospel message. We need to know the significance of the death and resurrection of Jesus and what it means to leave sin behind and become follow-ers of Christ. It's not enough to just encourage people to be good. We want our friends and family members to be saved—to be rescued from the domain of darkness and transformed into the Kingdom of light. The gospel has to be the center of our message.

MR. MATT NORTHRUP (high school dean): It's a difficult balancing act to develop relationships with nonbelievers without becoming friends of the world. Some Christians stay inside the "salt shaker" [the church] and don't have anyone in their lives who doesn't believe in Jesus. Other people are so immersed in our culture that they lose their ability to make positive changes. We need to pray for wisdom and guidance to know where the boundaries are. I definitely think that young ladies should make sure that their closest friends and mentors are Christians, and they should be supported by these friends. Their best friends should not be those they're trying to win for the Lord.

Have you shared your faith with a friend?

JON SALLADIN (student, age 15): I shared my faith with my friend Dominic when he spent the night. I asked him, "Hey, Dominic, have you ever accepted Jesus into your heart?" He said no, so I told him, "You should, because then you can go to heaven." He said that the whole religion thing wasn't for him, and that gave me a chance to explain how Christianity isn't a religion—it's a relationship with God. Dominic became more interested after I told him that. He hasn't accepted Christ yet, but I think he's on his way. Another way I witness is by example. I play football, and all the other players on the team have foul mouths. It doesn't matter whether they make a good or bad play, they'll use every word in the book. But when I make a bad play, I just shake it off and try again. I don't use cuss words.

JONATHAN YOUNKMAN (student, age 15): When I was in middle school, I was talking to my friend's little brother about Jesus on the school bus. I asked him if he'd ever prayed to receive Christ into his heart and he said he wasn't sure. So I shared the gospel with him and then we prayed together on the bus.

In what ways are you an example to those who are living by the world's standards?

SARAH UTTERBACK (student, age 16): I just started a new job, and although the place isn't "shady," most of the employees aren't Christians. They've started to realize that I'm different, because they've been asking me questions like, "Why are you so happy?" and "Why are you so smiley?" I've realized that I can be a witness for Christ by my example and through my actions. For instance, when coworkers ask, "What's that twinkle in your eye?" I tell them that I have a relationship with God. I've already begun to get labeled with comments like, "Oh, you're a church girl" and "You're a hard-core Christian." I smile in response and say, "Yes, I am." Yesterday I told a coworker that I'm a Christian, and he acted like it was a drag. I was able to explain that being a Christian is fun and cool—it's not a downer. So it's been a wake-up call for me to have people ask questions about why I'm different and to use those opportunities to share my faith.

ERIN DIEFENBACH (student, age 17): The friends I sit with at lunch know I'm a Christian, and they also know I attend a Christian club. I'm not ashamed of my beliefs—I try to set an example, and I share my faith when I can.

DAVID STRUM *(student, age 15): I don't have too many friends who aren't Christians, but one guy in my biology class at school is an atheist. One day he was making comments like, "There is no God" and "I hate people who believe in God." I tried to respond in a way that he could understand by saying, "Dude, you're an atheist, but it takes more faith to believe in atheism than Christianity. For instance, how do you prove amino acids became cells on their own?" He was speechless. I'm hoping he'll think about that to a greater extent and discover the truth.*

ALYSON THOMAS *(student, age 16): I'm on Facebook, but instead of writing about myself in the "About Me" section, I listed various Scriptures that have special meaning in my life. It's a good witnessing tool because whenever someone clicks on my profile, they notice right away that I'm a Christian. On a more personal level, my friends often come to me for advice because I'm good at listening. If they're going through a rough patch, I always point them to the Lord—I remind them how much He loves and cares for them and how special they are to Him. I try to use Scriptures and stories in the Bible that relate to their circumstances. A lot of people in the Bible went through difficulties, so I'll often use one of them as an example when I'm talking to a friend who's going through a tough time.*

MARY SPAGNOLA *(student, age 16): In eighth grade I went to a party and was surprised to see alcohol there. I went into another room to call my mom and asked her to pick me up. As it turned out, one of my friends who was at the party left with me. She said later that if I hadn't left, she wouldn't have had the courage to do it on her own.*

JONATHAN YOUNKMAN *(student, age 15): I try to live by example. I smile a lot, I pay attention to what I wear, and I keep my mouth clean—no profanity.* ❀

What Say You?

1) Jesus has called us to be His ambassadors, or representatives (see 2 Corinthians 5:20). What does that mean to you, and how does it relate to your life?

2) Are you comfortable sharing your Christian faith with others? If just the thought of it makes you nervous, take this moment to pray and ask God to give you greater courage. Then ask Him to give you an opportunity to talk to someone about Jesus!

3) Write down the name of someone who is a nonbeliever. Commit to pray for him or her, and think of some ways that you can be "salt and light" by your example.

Strength in Numbers

Check it out:

Proverbs 15:22

Whenever someone asks me if it's okay to bring an extra person to an event I'm hosting, I always give the same response: "Absolutely. The more the merrier!" Whether it's a party, a barbecue, an athletic activity, or a night on the town, it's fun to have as many people there as possible.

That's especially true in your teen years—a great time in life for building friendships. Not only are you regularly at school and church, which provide endless opportunities for interaction with peers, but the grown-up responsibilities of marriage, children, and a career are not on your radar yet. That freedom allows you to get involved in a number of social activities, such as school and church functions, sports, hobbies, volunteering, travel, and mission trips. Now is the ideal time to spread your wings and soar—to get in touch with who you are in Christ and begin to discover His plans for your future.

What is this time in your life not so good for? Getting tied down in an exclusive relationship. Are you aware that only a small percentage of high school sweethearts eventually marry? (I've even heard that the number is as low as one percent!) That means that if you have a boyfriend in your early teen years, you run a high risk of breaking up. I don't know about you, but with odds like that, I'd prefer to avoid a broken heart and remain footloose and fancy-free! Who needs a lot of unnecessary drama in life? As I once read in a comical ad, "Save the drama for your mama!"

I'm not suggesting you completely avoid the hotties you've been spying (I mean, can a girl exist without chocolate?), but I am encouraging you to get acquainted with guys outside of one-on-one dating relationships. Group activities and church functions are a healthier environment for developing male friendships. Social events give you the opportunity to spend time with guys while avoiding intimate settings that can lead to sexual pressure and heartache.

The voice of experience is talking here. When I was in high school and on through my twenties, I went out with mixed groups from my Bible study on the weekends. We would meet at a restaurant for dinner and do something fun afterward (like go to a movie, head to someone's house to play a game or watch a movie, go bowling, shoot some pool, or listen to live jazz at a coffeehouse). I was able to hang out with guys and get to know them in a relaxed environment. In many ways I was better off spending time with these friends instead of being immersed in the dating scene. No relationship insecurities, no heavy conversations or expectations—just some lighthearted fellowship with a bunch of cool people.

I still enjoy getting together with groups. Recently I went with a Sunday school class to see the latest Narnia film at the famous El Capitan Theatre in Hollywood. We went out to eat afterward and made a night of it. I had a great time.

There's no denying that dating can be fun too, but it adds some major drawbacks to the mix. Joshua Harris, who wrote the popular book *I Kissed Dating Goodbye*, offers these important facts about the downside to dating:

1. Dating leads to intimacy but not necessarily to commitment.
2. Dating tends to bypass the friendship stage of a relationship.
3. Dating can bring sexual temptation.
4. Dating often isolates a couple from other important relationships with family and friends.
5. Dating can distract young people from their primary responsibility of preparing for the future.

I think Josh brings up significant truths that should concern each of us who are single, at whatever age. Without question, dating brings pressures and complications that would otherwise not be present. Sexual temptation is one of the biggest hurdles. Most people only go out with others they're physically attracted to. When a guy and a girl are smitten with each other, they're bound to encounter some temptation when they spend time alone. The power of sexuality should never be underestimated. That's why some Christian teens avoid the dating scene altogether and hang out with friends instead. Others choose to date, but they make sure they are never alone with the person they're dating.

One guy told me that when he and his girlfriend first started going out, they made a commitment to always have someone else around. They didn't want to find themselves in a romantic setting that could heighten their emotions and lead to physical intimacy. I admire this couple for choosing to honor the Lord in their relationship. Their decision complies with 1 Thessalonians 4:3-6: "It is God's will that you should be sanctified [holy]: that you should avoid sexual immorality; that each of you should learn to control his own body in a way that is holy and honorable, not in passionate lust like the heathen, who do not know God; and that in this matter no one should wrong his brother or take advantage of him."

According to this Scripture, we need to put righteousness and purity above our sinful desires. We each have a responsibility to honor God and one another by abstaining from sexual immorality. That can be a challenge because physical contact is almost always progressive in nature. The more time you spend with a guy you like, the more familiar you are with one another, and the more liberties you will want to take. One thing can lead to another. That's the reason I titled this chapter "Strength in Numbers." It's a lot easier to abide by God's command to save yourself sexually for marriage when you have Christian friends who will provide accountability and back you up in your decision to remain pure.

If you and a guy like each other and want to spend time together apart from a social group, why not go to a restaurant or a public function like a concert or sporting event? That way you can do something fun while avoiding the temptation to compromise your standards. Sitting in a dark room watching a movie or parking the car in a secluded spot at night to have a "chat" are situations you should steer clear of (literally). God is never impressed by your willpower to abstain from sin—He expects you to run from it with full vigor. "Flee the evil desires of youth, and pursue righteousness, faith, love and peace, along with those who call on the Lord out of a pure heart" (2 Timothy 2:22).

Let me leave you with this final thought: God understands your need for emotional and physical intimacy; after all, He created you that way. If you'll abide by His commands and wait for His plan, you'll discover the very best He has to offer . . . all in His perfect time.

For now, how about rounding up your friends for a night of movies and ice cream? Or better yet, sundaes. Bring it on.

LET'S TALK ABOUT DATING

MR. AUSTIN SEFTON (youth leader): High school is not the time when most people find their husbands and wives, so if you're considering dating someone exclusively, ask yourself what your motive is.

ALYSON THOMAS (student, age 16): I've only been asked out once—in seventh grade—and I think the guy's friends put him up to it, because they were all hanging back, snickering and laughing. It made me feel horrible. I haven't been real trusting of guys after that experience. Besides, as a sixteen-year-old, I'm much too young to be thinking of marriage, and that's where dating is supposed to lead. For that reason, I'm holding off on dating until I'm old enough to get engaged and married.

DUSTY SANDERSON (student, age 17): I'm a "go with the flow" type of guy, so right now I don't have strong feelings about dating or not dating. I do know that I'm only interested in getting involved with someone who has qualities I would look for in a wife. I made the mistake of dating a non-Christian girl for a few months, and it made me realize that I never want to date someone outside my faith again. No matter how much I thought I had in common with that *girl at the beginning, I really had nothing in common because we saw the world completely differently. I wanted her to know God so much, but when I would talk to her about Him, she would say things like, "I don't believe that the Bible is God's Word—it was written by men." I couldn't relate to her when she made statements like that.*

JULIA SALLADIN (student, age 18): I really like boys and dating, but my first obligation is to the Lord. I've had two official relationships so far, and in both instances I was more focused on the guy than on God. For that reason I'm not going to allow myself to be in another relationship until I'm spiritually mature. I want to get to know the Lord better and discover His calling on my life.

Which is better—single dating or group dating?

MARY SPAGNOLA (student, age 16): As a rule, high school relationships don't last, so that's why it's better to wait until you're older before becoming serious with someone. The more you put into a relationship, the more it's going to hurt when it's over, so why invest a lot of emotional energy at this point in life? I like the idea of group dating much better. It's safer and more comfortable.

PASTOR LUKE CUNNINGHAM (youth minister): This is what I always say to a teen when he or she asks my advice about whether or not to start dating someone: "Are you looking to honor God with your life?" If they say yes, then I ask, "Are you looking to fool around physically and have sex?" They always say no. At that point I ask, "Well, then, what's the difference between a dating relationship and a good friendship?" I always get nothing in response. Society has put a

tag on dating that says that if you're going out with someone, it's a license to mess around physically. I encourage
teens to just have friends for this season of their lives. What
blows my mind are these "dating marriages" in high school,
where, for example, a fifteen-year-old boy has been dating a
girl since seventh grade, and he's quit sports and is working
so he has money to take her out. He has no friends—he only
interacts with her. That is so unhealthy, and nine times out of
ten there's sexual sin involved. Why would he do that when
he only gets to be a kid once? And on a spiritual level, he
can't honor God when he's given away his heart and everything else.

ERIN DIEFENBACH (student, age 17): At my age, group dating is better than one-on-one. I want to prepare myself for my
future husband by only "dating" Jesus right now. I think it's
important to develop a healthy relationship with Him before
trying to have a healthy relationship with a guy. I also think
that if I'm stable in the Lord, I will have a clearer perspective
to know whether or not a guy is worth investing in.

CHRISTIAN TURNER (student, age 16): I don't have a problem asking a girl to a school dance, where it's a big social
function in a nonthreatening environment. That type of setting feels comfortable to me at this stage of my life—just
talking to a girl and getting to know her in a mixed group.

JULIA SALLADIN (student, age 18): In both of my dating
relationships, I started going out with the guys one week
after meeting them. I was never able to see how they inter-
acted with people in a group setting. Also, it would have
been a good idea to find out what my friends and family
thought, but I didn't seek their counsel. So the next time

I consider dating someone, I want to become friends with him first and take time to discover if he's someone I might want to marry. If so, then I'll get to know him on a personal level. Dating isn't supposed to be just for fun—it's supposed to help you find someone to spend the rest of your life with.

SAMANTHA BOWSER (student, age 17): I like the idea of hanging out in groups because it allows you to get to know a guy in a relaxed environment. Conversation comes easier too—you're more natural than you would be one-on-one at a restaurant. Another positive aspect of being in a group is that it keeps you from doing things that you might be tempted to do if you and a guy are alone.

SARAH UTTERBACK (student, age 16): In my past relationship with my boyfriend, we started off as friends for six months, then we group dated for another six months before we became exclusive. Even though our relationship didn't work out, I think we approached dating the right way. Because we were friends at the beginning, we understood each other's personality and relationship with the Lord, and we also observed how the other person acted around their friends.

FRANKIE OGAZ (student, age 16): They say that love is "friendship on fire," so I think it's wise to start with group dating. If you like each other, you can gradually transition into single dating, and by then you'll know more about what you want from the relationship.

PASTOR JONATHAN LAKES (youth minister): Hanging out in groups is a safer route during the teen years. However, I dated one-on-one when I was in high school, and I held true to my morals and convictions because my faith was important to me.

MR. AUSTIN SEFTON (youth leader): I dated a girl throughout my junior and senior year of high school, and we were both actively involved in our church youth group. When we broke up, it hurt the chemistry of our group—it was never the same, even though it was still good. My friendships with other girls in the group became awkward because a lot of them were her friends. I also didn't like to see my guy friends interacting with my ex-girlfriend. Knowing what I know now, I should have prayed about that relationship before jumping into it. The decision to become involved with someone is spiritual, just like any other decision in life. It needs to be backed up with prayer and advice from spiritual mentors. ❀

What Say You?

1) Name a few activities you enjoy doing with friends.

2) What are your strategies for resisting sexual temptation?

3) Think of some ways you and your friends can provide accountability for one another. Why not arrange to get together with them this week to discuss your ideas?

He's Not into You? Next!

Check it out:

Proverbs 4:23

A friend told me something that blew me away. Her fifteen-year-old daughter, Hayley, went to summer camp and created a little game with the guys: she would spot a cute guy and casually walk by, smile at him, and keep walking. Then she would count in her head how many seconds it took him to run up and start a conversation with her.

Hello!? Can you relate to that? Me neither! It's totally unfair that girls like Hayley can call their own shots. Most of us have never played Hayley's little game of catch-me-if-you-can, and we couldn't if we tried. We often find guys' signals to be complicated, confusing, and downright frustrating.

Do you know a girl like Hayley who always seems to capture male attention? Of course you do. She may not be drop-dead gorgeous or Miss Congeniality, but she has a style and demeanor that draw the guys to her like dancing mice to a pied piper. Guys are always checking her out. When they aren't doing that, they're trying to impress her or engage her in conversation. Let's face it: when it comes to attracting guys, this cool chick is most likely to succeed.

Would you like to know one of the main reasons why? Okay, girls, I'm going to level with you, so scoot a little closer in your chairs. Guy magnets like Hayley, although few and far between, are successful because they don't try to get attention in an obvious way. They aren't at home texting plan A and plan B to their girlfriends on their cells. They don't conveniently hang out near their heartthrobs' lockers or try to make eye contact—holding their gaze for three seconds (like that would ever work)! They don't attempt to be overheard having a giggly good time with their girlfriends or quipping clever lines. Most of all, they never send friends on a mission to leak their "guess who likes you?" secrets to their crushes. These guy magnets just look good, let their personalities shine, and allow the chips to fall where they may.

Does attempting to capture a guy's attention *ever* work? Yes, it does, but it's usually when you both share a mutual attraction. For example, when my parents were in college, they spotted each other in the cafeteria and played a little cat-and-mouse game with their eyes. My dad-to-be kept glancing at my future mom and looking away, and she responded in kind. It obviously paid off, or I wouldn't be sitting here writing this book! The reason the eye contact game was successful for them was because there was mutual chemistry. If my dad-to-be had not been attracted to the girl who was to become my mom, he might have been flattered by her batting eyes but most likely would have set his sights on someone else.

I realize it's tough when you have a crush on someone who doesn't share your romantic feelings. I've been there, and it's torturous. But what I've learned through the agony is to give up the chase. I've accepted that some guys are going to think I'm cute and others won't look twice at me.

That's okay. I just allow guys who are interested to take the initiative, and I try to avoid getting caught in fantasies involving the ones who don't share my attraction.

It comes down to this: every guy has a specific "look" he's initially drawn to. The guy you're interested in has to be attracted to *your* face, *your* smile, *your* hair, *your* eye color, and *your* body shape. If your appearance doesn't do it for him, don't take it personally. There will be other guys who think you're gorgeous. It's all about perception. As one male member of a panel discussion at a single women's conference stated, "Regardless of what size or shape your backside is, I guarantee that *some* guy is diggin' it!"

Here's a good example of the concept of perception: one of my male friends told me he walked into a pastry shop with two of his buddies, and one of them (a handsome dude, by the way) went nuts for a girl behind the counter. This smitten Romeo kept whispering how gorgeous the bakery babe was, but my friend and his other buddy were wondering what he saw in her—they thought she looked rather plain. Case in point: beauty is in the eye of the beholder.

As with every rule, there are exceptions. Not all attraction occurs instantaneously; sometimes it grows with time. A guy might develop an interest in you after getting acquainted and spending hours in your company. That's always a possibility, but this chapter isn't about possibilities—it's about *probabilities*. Because I've had more experience in this game than you, I know what it's like to work hard to attract someone's attention. I've also witnessed some of my friends trying to do the same thing. Here's what I've learned: nine times out of ten it doesn't work! If a guy isn't into you to begin with, there isn't much you can do to cause him to spring into hot pursuit. Either he's attracted to you or he isn't. Plain and simple. Even if you manage to capture your heartthrob's attention, you'll probably discover he lacks the level of enthusiasm you wish he had. This often results in what I refer to as the "wandering eye syndrome." In plain English, it means that although he's sitting with you, he's also checking out somebody else!

The best advice I can give is to not waste time on fantasies. Think of all the friends you know who've had major crushes—I bet you can count on one hand how many actually got a relationship out of it. It's a waste of emotional energy.

Don't just take my word for it. As with every issue in life, the Bible has something to say about this subject. Proverbs 4:23 clearly states: "Above all else, guard your heart, for it is the wellspring of life."

These years of your life have enough challenges without adding potential "guy trauma" to the mix. When you put your heart on the line, you risk suffering one of the worst types of pain: rejection. The Lord understands this, and that's why He instructs you to protect your heart like the precious entity it is. He wants to spare you from stepping on emotional land mines that will leave you broken and scarred.

If you currently have a crush on someone who isn't showing an interest in you, just admire him from a distance and accept defeat. Don't attempt to manipulate the situation. Hold out for that true love who will appreciate the beautiful girl you are, inside and out. And above all else, guard your heart!

"Teach me your way, O LORD, and I will walk in your truth; give me an undivided heart, that I may fear your name" (Psalm 86:11).

LET'S TALK ABOUT CRUSHES

MARIN JOHNSEN (student, age 15): I think there's a difference between thinking a guy is cute and having a full-blown crush. I try not to develop a crush on a guy unless I can tell he's got a thing for me first. There are strategies you can use if you're stuck on someone who doesn't like you in return. You can spend more time with your friends and family so they will distract you from thinking about him. You can ask God to help you stop fantasizing, and you can discipline your mind.

BECCA YOUNKMAN (student, age 17): If a guy you're attracted to doesn't feel the same way about you, try to focus on things about him that you don't admire.

JENNA SALLADIN (student, age 17): My girlfriend and I both liked the same guy, and then he started liking her. I dealt with that by busying myself with friends and with other things. Now I only think of him as a friend.

ELISSA MASON (student, age 14): I'll be talking to friends at school, and everyone will be asking each other, "Who do you like?" I'm not the type of person who's always interested in a guy, but my friends say, "You have to like someone—you have to have feelings for someone." I disagree with that. Girls get too caught up with liking guys. If they're constantly seeking that attention, then maybe they're not getting enough of it at home or they're not spending quality time with God.

BECCA YOUNKMAN (student, age 17): One of my girlfriends was bummed for a couple of weeks because guys weren't paying attention to her, and then a guy started talking to her and she was happy again. I asked her about *it, and she said, "I kinda feast off of guys. I thrive off of the attention they give me." I was thinking,* That is so unhealthy.

MRS. KRISTIN SALLADIN *(home educators co-op director): Some people who have intense crushes tend to crave drama in their lives. A girl will think,* He's looking at me! He's talking to me! *And then the guy won't pay attention to her, and she's in the depths of despair. Crushes feel safer than relationships, because in real relationships you have to work.*

MR. TIMOTHY STRANSKE *(high school teacher): Girls need to put their trust in the Lord and not in teenage boys, who are about the worst thing to depend upon during the adolescent years.*

MR. AUSTIN SEFTON *(youth leader): It's easy to become obsessed with someone you're attracted to. When I was dating a girl a few years ago, my whole mind was consumed with her and my focus was not on the Lord. If we aren't seeking Christ more fervently than the person we're attracted to, then we have a problem. Jesus should be our number one.*

GUYS ONLY: *What do you think about a girl when you find out she likes you but you don't share her attraction?*

BEN TRAPP (student, age 15): There was a girl who liked me and said it to my face, but it totally turned me off because I wasn't attracted to her. I think it might be better for girls to hide their crushes, because sometimes they can be overly aggressive. Another girl told me that the only way I could see her is if we were boyfriend and girlfriend. And I was thinking, Okay, well, bye! *At that point I knew she wasn't hanging around me because she wanted to be my friend— it was only because she had a crush on me. Another thing*

I don't appreciate is when girls send me a bunch of text messages. Delete, delete, delete.

JONATHAN YOUNKMAN (student, age 15): If a girl likes me, I try to be nice without leading her on. Last year during PE, a girl walked by and told me I was cute and kept walking. I really didn't know what to say in response except, "Thanks." Her statement kinda caught me off guard.

DUSTY SANDERSON (student, age 17): If a girl likes me, that's fine. But if she ever came on too strong, I would say to her, "I don't want to hurt you, but I don't view you as a potential girlfriend. I just want to be friends."

GUYS ONLY: *What is the best way for a girl to capture your attention?*

DAVID STRUM (student, age 15): I think a girl should become friends with me first and then see what happens as our friendship grows.

DUSTY SANDERSON (student, age 17): If a girl likes me, it's okay if she wants to introduce herself. I wouldn't be turned off or intimidated by that. One thing I've noticed is that sometimes when I'm nice to a girl and talk to her, she automatically assumes that I think of her as more than a friend or that I'm leading her on.

JONATHAN YOUNKMAN (student, age 15): If a girl was being too forceful, I would stay away from her. But if she played it cool and just hung out and didn't pressure me, then I might start liking her.

MATT GODSHALL (student, age 14): If a girl liked me and I didn't know her, then she would need to get over her self-consciousness and talk to me so I would know she exists. That sounds like a no-brainer, but I know a lot of girls who like different guys and are too afraid to talk to them.

GUYS ONLY: *What would you think about a girl asking you out?*

PAUL HONTZ (student, age 19): I'd prefer not to have that happen, but ultimately it depends on the situation.

DUSTY SANDERSON (student, age 17): I'm not really in favor of a girl asking me to a dance or a formal. I'd prefer to ask her instead. Right now at my school, the Sadie Hawkins dance is coming up (where girls ask the guys), and it's kinda scary because I don't know who's going to invite me to be her date. I prefer dances where the guys do the asking. But if a girl does ask me to a dance, then I think she should be someone I know pretty well.

CHRISTIAN TURNER (student, age 16): I'm uncomfortable with Sadie Hawkins dances. I think it comes down to that natural instinct a guy has for wanting to be the initiator and provider. When I'm not able to initiate, it sort of feels like I'm not doing my job right.

GUYS ONLY: *What should a girl never do to try to get a guy?*

MATT GODSHALL (student, age 14): A guy likes the thrill of the chase, so a girl shouldn't make it totally obvious that she likes him. It would be better for him to want her to like him. Keep the intrigue going.

DUSTY SANDERSON (student, age 17): She shouldn't go outside her moral boundaries, such as dressing sexy and using her sexuality.

JONATHAN YOUNKMAN (student, age 15): Don't wear skanky, immodest clothes.

JON SALLADIN (student, age 15): She shouldn't be superficial. For instance, even though I'm really into football, a girl shouldn't pretend that she's into it just to impress me. She should be herself.

BEN TRAPP (student, age 15): If a girl says she's a Christian, then I'm going to watch her actions. If she parties, for instance, I'll definitely see that she's not being genuine and honest. ❀

What Say You?

1) Are you willing to accept that some guys whom you're attracted to won't share your feelings?

2) What are some things you can do to avoid wasting time on fantasies?

3) If you currently have a crush on someone, how are you dealing with it? Have you sought direction from the Lord?

Ditching the Ditch

Check it out:

Proverbs 3:21-23

I've never been enthusiastic about Internet dating. I know everyone seems to be doing it these days and there's no stigma attached to it anymore, but it still feels a little weird to me.

For one thing, I've always hoped that when someone asks me how I met my future spouse, I'd have something more intriguing to say than "We met online." Then there's the whole self-advertising campaign that goes along with Internet dating. The girls try to impress the guys with lines like, "People tell me I'm a great gourmet cook, and I love watching football!" Guys try to appeal to the ladies by tapping into their romantic side: "I love candlelight dinners and walks on moonlit beaches." (How original! Who doesn't like to go out to eat and walk on the beach!)

It's for these reasons among others that when it comes to online dating, I'd rather not. But when the founder of one of the largest Internet dating services offered me a *free* subscription, I was only too thrilled to accept his generous offer! So I filled out the two-hour personality profile, posted three flattering photos of myself, and opened my site for "dating business."

After corresponding with a few ho-hum guys, a honey named Matt popped up on my computer screen. Not only was he cute—complete with a dimple in his chin—but he identified himself as a committed Christian, which was the strongest appeal. Matt and I cruised through the stages of communication, and before long, our mutual attraction took off like a Learjet speeding down the run-way! The e-mails were getting longer, and the late-night phone calls were lasting three to four hours. The more I got to know Matt, the more I liked him. He was funny, intelligent, into cars and computers—which I found intriguing—and he was the best writer of any guy I knew (with the exception of my dad). I also liked the fact that he didn't know my last name, which was kind of cool for the time being.

Since Matt and I lived far from each other, we agreed to get together for the first time at an upcoming event I was going to attend that was close to his hometown. So I e-mailed him some details about the trip, feeling very excited about the prospect of meeting him in person, and . . . poof! I never heard from him again.

You might find this hard to believe, considering I didn't get an opportunity to meet Matt face-to-face, but I took his sudden disappearance really hard. The way he cut off com-munication so abruptly was heartless! He offered no expla-nation, no good-bye, no closure—just a sudden amputation of his presence. He probably met another girl and didn't have the courage to tell me, but it would have been consid-erate of him to say or write *something*. As it was, I was left to fight my hurt feelings cold turkey after having become emotionally involved. And, believe me, getting over him didn't happen overnight.

A month after Matt disappeared into cyberspace, I instant messaged him a few lines to say hello and to verify to myself that he was still on the map. He responded with one word: "Hi!" and a smiley face. At that point, I received a confirmation to what I already knew: "The plane had flown into the side of the mountain—no survivors—call off the search."

For the past year I haven't been interested or involved with anyone, and I've been loving the tranquility. No drama, no pain, no insecurities—just a smooth and easy ride. Do I intend to stay single forever? No. But for the moment I'm enjoying the freedom that comes from being romantically detached.

Now don't get me wrong—I adore the opposite sex! Some of my best memories have involved guys on some level. They've added a lot of interest, fun, and comedy to my life, occasionally making me giggle to the point that I couldn't swallow my beverage. (What happens when a person is laughing too hard to gulp down a mouthful of soda pop? Yep. You guessed it!)

Although I've had some great times with guys over the years, I'd rather not focus on smiles and warm fuzzies in this chapter (I doubt you need advice on how to have fun with guys anyway). No, it's more important to concentrate on avoiding the pitfalls.

I'd like you to visualize the following scenario: You're driving ninety miles per hour down the highway with the radio blaring, and you see me standing on the side of the road waving two red flags in your direction. I'm doing that because I know there's a ditch in the distance, and I'm trying to spare you from soaring through the air and taking a nose-dive into it. So I frantically wave the flags up and down, hoping you'll slow down long enough for me to warn you of the upcoming danger, and provide you with an alternate route.

That visual is another way of saying I'd like to help you avoid my mistakes. You see, I've plowed into that dating ditch more than once, and I've crawled out with a broken heart and a crushed spirit. I thank God regularly for His promise in Psalm 34:17-18: "The righteous cry out, and the LORD hears them; he delivers them from all their troubles. The LORD is close to the brokenhearted and saves those who are crushed in spirit." And yes, He did save me! But I still bear the scars from the pain of the past. I'm hoping those scars can serve a purpose in protecting you from similar heartaches.

My hope for this book is to provide you with friendship and "big sister advice." So as your adopted big sister, I'd like to pass along what I've learned about a variety of subjects, including dating and relationships. Here's the best advice I can offer, condensed into what I call the "three Ps of prevention":

Pray for guidance. When you develop an attraction for someone, it's easy to get lost in the clouds and rely solely on emotions to guide you. Very risky! Just as a pilot must depend on instruments to help him soar with confidence, so you must rely on more than feelings to help you succeed in your endeavors. That's why prayer is so important. God knows everything, and He sees the big picture. By seeking His will through prayer, you'll go beyond your limited knowledge to discover His infinite wisdom.

If you want to develop discernment, the Bible has a lot to offer too. For example, the book of Proverbs instructs you on such things as what kind of guy to look for (a kind man [see Proverbs 11:17] and a man who fears the Lord [see Proverbs 14:16]) and whom to avoid (a sluggard [see Proverbs 13:4], a hot-tempered man [see Proverbs 22:24-25], and one who is stingy [see Proverbs 23:6-7]).

When I was communicating with Matt, I expressed gratitude to the Lord for bringing an awesome guy (so I thought) into my life, but I should have been seeking spiritual discernment and guidance at the same time. If I had been more discerning about his character, I might have saved myself a lot of grief.

The Lord longs to show us His will, but we're often too distracted to find out what it is, or we don't want to know the answer because it might turn out to be the opposite of what we desire. It's always to our benefit to seek God's direction in every situation! He has our best interests in mind, and He has promised to lead us down the right road: "Trust in the LORD with all your heart and lean not on your own understanding; in all your ways acknowledge him, and he will make your paths straight" (Proverbs 3:5-6).

Protect your heart. We already covered this concept in the previous chapter, but it bears repeating. Let's review Proverbs 4:23: "Above all else, guard your heart, for it is the wellspring of life." You may have no control over a lot of things, but fortunately your heart isn't one of them. God has given you the ability to exercise willpower by keeping your emotions in check. You can't always safeguard yourself from a broken heart, but you can control its intensity by keeping your "heart guards" up as best you can.

Proceed with caution. In other words, go slow! It's not easy to put on the brakes in a romantic friendship when you long to spend every waking moment with someone you're crazy about, but if you want to save yourself a lot of pain down the line, hold back the desire to forge ahead. You don't want to spend an exorbitant amount of time with a guy, fall in love, and suffer a meltdown when the fairy tale ends. It's best to keep your eyes on the Lord and watch His signals closely. If you don't have peace about moving forward in a relationship, it's possible God is telling you that you're about to make a mistake. Take note!

So there you have it—my prescription for reducing your odds of a broken heart. Romantic relationships are fun and exciting, but they can also be reckless, landing you upside down in that dreaded ditch! That's why it's essential to pray and exercise judgment right from the start. With the Lord's help (and the "three Ps of prevention"), you can discover an alternate route to a place of tranquility. "This is my prayer: that your love may abound more and more in knowledge and depth of insight, so that you may be able to discern what is best and may be pure and blameless until the day of Christ" (Philippians 1:9-10).

LET'S TALK ABOUT HEARTBREAK

BECCA YOUNKMAN (student, age 17): It's important to make sure a guy is pursuing you with godly intentions. I've heard it said that a guy should be so close to God that you have to see God in order to see the guy.

ELISSA MASON (student, age 14): Girls are so much more emotional than guys, so even holding hands can make a girl feel emotionally attached. A guy might think, Whatever—I held your hand. No big deal. *We as females need to be cautious before doing things that will make us emotionally vulnerable. Also, don't accept anything a guy says*

*through texting and e-mails that he hasn't told you in person.
He could be sending you all sorts of flattering words but
then copying them to other girls.*

MR. AUSTIN SEFTON *(youth leader): When a girl is emotionally attached to a guy—confiding in him and sharing her
heart—it makes me a little nervous. I'm not just referring to
dating relationships but platonic friendships as well. When
it comes to disclosing personal information, I think it might
be best to talk to a Christian leader or a female friend rather
than a guy. I don't think most teen guys are at an age where
they can handle classified information in a mature way.*

PASTOR LUKE CUNNINGHAM *(youth minister): Don't
trust your feelings over your faith. Every week we deal
with girls who have boyfriends who call them names, treat
them poorly, yet still get to mess around with them physically. These girls are left thinking,* Maybe he still loves me,
*because they're following their feelings. Don't fall for the
lines that some guys use, such as, "I love you" and "You're
beautiful." Keep your emotions in check. Jeremiah 17:9
says, "The heart is deceitful above all things and beyond
cure. Who can understand it?"*

MRS. KRISTIN SALLADIN *(home educators co-op director):
Guys have a need for respect, but they should be showing
respect to girls too. If a guy isn't treating a girl right, then
she shouldn't accept that. One thing a girl can do to encourage a guy to be a gentleman is to act like a lady. By doing
so, a girl is giving a nonverbal message that says, "This is
my standard, and this is how I expect to be treated."*

DUSTY SANDERSON *(student, age 17): I don't think there's
any way to keep from feeling sad and hurt when someone*

ends a relationship with you, but the best way to deal with it is to show respect for yourself and the other person.

BECCA YOUNKMAN (student, age 17): This guy and I liked each other, and for a while he opened doors for me and walked me to places, but when the relationship slowed down, he stopped doing those things. He shouldn't have acted like a gentleman just because he liked me—he should be that way all the time.

MARIN JOHNSEN (student, age 15): Watch how a guy treats his mom, because that's how he's going to treat his spouse. Also, if you're in a relationship, go to your parents for advice—especially your mom. I've compared my relationships with guys to those of my girlfriends, and mine have gone much smoother because I've talked to my mom a lot. She gives me great advice! Some of my friends don't talk to their moms at all, but they should because their moms know a lot more than they do.

MR. MATT NORTHRUP (high school dean): In my experience of working on a high school campus, I've seen countless couples devastated by extremely painful breakups. I've watched couples becoming more exclusive, and they begin to isolate themselves from their church as well as their friends and families. Dangers can occur in relationships when couples begin spending the majority of their free time together, away from their friends and families. It's essential for teens to have a support group, so I recommend that they hang out in large groups instead of pairing off in dating relationships. A girl can still get to know that special guy in a group setting, and it's actually better that way because she's able to observe how he relates to other people, and she can see whether or not he possesses the strong virtues and character qualities she's looking for.

Have you experienced a heartbreak? If so, what did you learn?

SARAH UTTERBACK (student, age 16): Recently my boyfriend and I broke up after dating for more than one year. It was really painful for me—I was a wreck for a period of time, but I'm doing much better now. What I learned through the process was that I was so focused on my boyfriend when we were together that I put my friendships on hold. It took breaking up with him to realize how much support I have in other people and how precious they are. Right now I'm enjoying being able to concentrate on my friends, especially my best girlfriend. We've been having so much fun together. As far as my ex-boyfriend and I are concerned, we weren't communicating well toward the end. He accused me of being too clingy, but I hadn't really changed from how I was before—it just started to bother him. If I get into another relationship, I'm going to work harder at guarding my heart, because I really got hurt.

JULIA SALLADIN (student, age 18): I've never had romantic relationships that weren't painful on some level. All through middle school and my freshman and sophomore years, I had crushes on guys and guys had crushes on me, and it was never very fulfilling. It's easy for a girl to spend a lot of time dwelling on boys, but then she ends up making decisions based around them instead of asking herself questions such as, Is this pleasing to God? and Is it healthy?

CHRISTIAN TURNER *(student, age 16): A broken heart can bring you closer to the Lord because it forces you to focus on Him through your pain. When I've gone through my alone times, I've realized that God is the true lover of my soul. He is the only one who's going to give me the intimacy I crave.*

JENNA SALLADIN *(student, age 17): This guy and I didn't officially date, but we liked each other, and I gave my heart to him. We were apart last summer, and during those months things changed. Now we aren't even friends. To make matters worse, he started pursuing one of my best friends, so now there's a strain between me and my friend. I didn't guard my heart, and I got hurt.* ✿

What Say You?

1) Have you plowed into the romance ditch in the past? If so, what did you learn from that experience?

2) Why do you think the Lord wants you to trust Him more than your own heart (see Proverbs 3:5-6; 28:26)?

3) When the next attractive guy displays an interest in you, what are some ways you can guard your heart (see Proverbs 4:23)?

Wait Up!

Check it out:

Romans 6:11-12

Tyler and Ashley never intended to have sex. They both came from solid Christian families and church backgrounds, and they respected God's command for sexual purity before marriage. When they began dating in college, they agreed that they would never go too far in their physical relationship. So how was it possible that they wound up sleeping together? What went wrong?

Let's go back to that first paragraph. Can you spot the downfall in Tyler and Ashley's relationship? Maybe you caught it the first time. Here's the glitch: By becoming physically involved, Tyler and Ashley opened the door to a lot of pressure and temptation. Even though they sincerely wanted to abstain from sexual immorality, they set themselves up for failure.

As I mentioned in the previous chapter, physical expression is progressive. A nice long kiss that leaves a guy and girl starry-eyed is not going to satisfy them two weeks down the line. It will take more "action" to produce the same level of excitement. That's just the way human beings are wired.

A couple can convince themselves and each other that they're not going to go too far sexually, but if they're making out on a regular basis with hands roaming in all directions, they're putting their willpower to the test. For Tyler and Ashley, their resistance collapsed.

Here's the rest of their true story. After only a few sexual encounters, Ashley got pregnant. It was a traumatic situation for both her and Tyler as they broke the news to family and friends (many of whom grieved at the announcement) and had to make some hasty decisions. A short engagement was set, and Ashley and her mother worked around the clock to plan the rushed wedding. After the bride and groom said their vows, they moved into an apartment and found life and their new marriage extremely challenging as they tried to adjust to living with one another, dealing with Ashley's pregnancy and medical bills, preparing for the baby to arrive, and sacrificing to keep Tyler in school. As far as Ashley's dream of graduating from college, well, that had to wait.

More than a decade has passed since then, and Tyler and Ashley now have additional children and a much more stable home life. Although they sought and received forgiveness from God for their past sin, there is one consequence they cannot escape: they will always regret having had premarital sex. The short-term pleasure was not worth the long-term pain and inconvenience they've suffered. One of the hardest realities is that they cannot tell their children they waited until their wedding night to give each other the precious gift of sex. Tyler and Ashley cheated themselves out of God's best plan for their marriage. If only they had done it His way.

I heard a pastor say that there isn't one Christian couple who engages in premarital sex who doesn't end up regretting it at some point. That's because God's moral law of abstinence (holding out for sex until marriage) was designed for our own protection. If we violate that command, we place ourselves in harm's way.

In Southern California where I live, the Los Angeles Police Department has some clever slogans to encourage citizens to make lawful decisions:

"Click It or Ticket" (for not wearing a seat belt)
"Over the Limit, Under Arrest" (for excess alcohol consumption)
"Three Strikes, You're Out" (for criminal charges)

These unique messages are another way of saying, "Obey the law or suffer the consequences." Did the justice system develop these regulations for the purpose of being cruel and infringing on our privileges? No. The laws that require us to wear seat belts, to not drink and drive, and to avoid criminal charges were set up for our protection and the safety of others.

The same is true of God's commands. In His Word, He has instructed us in the way we should go (see Psalm 32:8), and it benefits us if we are obedient.

Tyler and Ashley violated one of God's moral laws and ended up with an unplanned pregnancy. There are other people who have suffered worse consequences for the sin of sexual immorality. One girl told me that before she was a Christian she had casual sex with a male friend. Of course, the guy didn't inform her that he had herpes simplex (a sexually transmitted disease). She contracted the virus and is now stuck with it for the rest of her life. (There is no cure for a viral infection, although plenty of hit movies and TV shows that glamorize premarital sex won't tell you that.)

Am I sharing these stories to frighten you? No, I'm just

being real. The fact is that more than twenty sexually transmitted diseases exist currently, and they are at epidemic proportions. The only way to guarantee that you won't contract one (or more) is by honoring the Lord with your body. So what does the Bible say you should do? "Flee from sexual immorality. All other sins a man commits are outside his body, but he who sins sexually sins against his own body. Do you not know that your body is a temple of the Holy Spirit, who is in you, whom you have received from God? You are not your own; you were bought at a price. Therefore honor God with your body" (1 Corinthians 6:18-20).

When you invited Christ into your heart, you accepted His free gift of eternal life that was purchased by His blood on the cross. That means that the Holy Spirit now dwells within you, and your name is recorded in the Lamb's Book of Life for all time (see Revelation 21:27). You belong to God in both body and spirit. Therefore, as the above Scripture states, you have a responsibility to honor Him with your body by avoiding sexual sin.

Sexual intimacy in marriage is one of God's greatest gifts to humans. It is the physical and spiritual expression of committed love, whereby husband and wife become one flesh (see Mark 10:6-9). The only way to experience sex in the fullness of how God intended it is by abiding by His moral code. That requires a predetermined effort to resist temptation and wait for His perfect plan. There is no other alternative!

If you haven't already made a sincere commitment to abstain sexually before marriage, will you do so now? I'm not referring to a compromise that allows you to fool around without crossing the line—the whole "technical virgin" bit. I'm talking about a decision to pursue righteousness—denying yourself the pleasures of the moment to live a pure life before God.

If you're looking for accountability (and I recommend it), there's a Christian ministry that's designed to encourage moral purity. It's called True Love Waits—maybe you're already familiar with it. This youth-based international campaign challenges teens to make a commitment to sexual abstinence before marriage. Since its origin in 1993, more than 3 million pledges have been made by young people around the world! If you would like to add your name to the list by filling out a commitment card, visit http://www.truelovewaits.com. Through the Web site, you'll also find newsletters, conference information, and merchandise for sale, such as the popular True Love Waits ring.

If you've already fallen into sexual sin, take heart! You, too, have the opportunity to make a purity pledge. Jesus Christ offers forgiveness to anyone who sincerely asks for it: "I will forgive [your] wickedness and will remember [your] sins no more" (Hebrews 8:12). You can start anew by being cleansed and restored through His saving grace!

Are you ready to surrender *everything* to the Lord, including your desires for physical intimacy? That will be one of the wisest decisions you'll ever make.

LET'S TALK ABOUT WAITING FOR SEX

FRANKIE OGAZ (student, age 16): As Christians, we should keep our conscience clear, so as the saying goes, "Let your conscience be your guide." If you think a certain situation might create temptation, don't even go there. Be careful who you choose to spend time with, watch what you wear, and pray for willpower.

CHRISTIAN TURNER (student, age 16): It's important not to create an intimate environment, such as sitting in a dark room with someone and watching a movie. Always make sure there are other people around. It would be a good idea to have an accountability partner too. My dad is my accountability partner—he and I are really close.

ERIN DIEFENBACH (student, age 17): When couples get into sexual relationships, a common saying is, "I just didn't see it coming." That's why it's really important to have a strong mind-set ahead of time.

SAMANTHA BOWSER (student, age 17): Abstinence is really important to me. I've never been confronted with sexual temptation up to this point because I've tried to avoid it.

PAUL HONTZ (student, age 19): I have four sisters, so a question that I've asked myself in the past is, Would it be okay if a guy who was dating one of my sisters was fooling around with her? That helps to keep things in perspective.

DUSTY SANDERSON (student, age 17): I think it's important not only to make a decision not to have sex before marriage but also to understand your reasons why. For me, I know God commands us to reserve sex for marriage, so I made a decision a long time ago to abide by that. It's a nonissue, so I don't feel as much pressure. Also, I know that sex is going to be extra special for me when I get married, and I don't want to ruin that.

SARAH UTTERBACK (student, age 16): I think it's a good idea to not only make a commitment to God and to yourself about your boundaries, but also to let the guy in on it.

He needs to know where your limit line is, and you need to know his.

MR. AUSTIN SEFTON (youth leader): Flee from sexual sin, as Joseph did when Potiphar's wife grabbed his cloak and said, "Come to bed with me" [Genesis 39:7]. Joseph didn't stand there and think, I'm going to be strong, and she won't be able to seduce me. No, Joseph hauled out of there fast! He knew that sexual sin is a sin nobody has total control over.

PASTOR JONATHAN LAKES (youth minister): Girls are emotionally wired, and guys are physically wired. Therefore, guys need to guard themselves by not feeding their sexual desires. Likewise, girls need to be conscientious about not talking, dressing, or acting in ways that might encourage guys in their desires. Accountability needs to be established on both fronts. I remind the students in my youth group of Mark 12:30, which says, "Love the Lord your God with all your heart and with all your soul and with all your mind and with all your strength."

Do you know someone who has suffered as a consequence of sexual sin?

MATT GODSHALL (student, age 14): One of my female friends didn't want to become sexually active, but after she had been dating her boyfriend for a year, he threatened to break up with her if she didn't give in. She wasn't in a good place in her relationship with the Lord at the time, so she fell into sexual sin and ended up getting pregnant and having a miscarriage. After that happened, she didn't want to continue that lifestyle, so she broke up with her boyfriend and came back to God.

DUSTY SANDERSON (student, age 17): I have a Christian friend who got his girlfriend pregnant. It really hurt his family. He ended up breaking up with the girl, and they put the baby up for adoption. Even though I'm sure my friend asked God for forgiveness, he really messed things up for himself and his future relationships.

What do you think about kissing?

CHRISTIAN TURNER (student, age 16): I think kissing is one of those things that puts a foot in the door for temptation. For me, I choose not to engage in kissing at this time in my life because I can eliminate a variable that way. I won't have to deal with potential problems that might occur.

SAMANTHA BOWSER (student, age 17): Kissing is a nice way of showing affection, and I don't see anything wrong with it as long as it stops there.

PAUL HONTZ (student, age 19): I think that kissing is okay, but it's not something that I want to just give away without thinking about it.

FRANKIE OGAZ (student, age 16): I want to limit myself to only kissing a guy on the cheek, except if it's a special moment. I want things to move really slow.

MRS. MEGAN BARBER (middle school teacher): At the public school where I teach, I see girls running after the things of the world and giving away pieces of themselves to guys that they'll never be able to get back. It's popular to go after the hottest guys and to hold hands and give kisses, hugs, and even more than that. It causes me to feel very heavyhearted. Those are pieces of a treasure that are meant for one man.

I want to see a girl save that treasure for someone deserving who will be blessed by it instead of giving away a piece here and there until she's left with an empty treasure chest, yet still wants to be treated like a treasure.

ALYSON THOMAS (student, age 16): I really don't want to kiss a guy until I'm in a serious relationship or engaged. Kissing is a form of commitment, and I don't want to give that away to just anybody. I think of it as giving a little piece of my heart, and I want to reserve all I can for my future husband. Here's an example of something along those lines: Two teachers at my school—both Christians—just got engaged recently. I thought it was really cool when I found out they didn't say "I love you" to each other until the night they got engaged.

SARAH UTTERBACK (student, age 16): Kissing is intimate. There's a certain point when it's no longer innocent, and you know when it's reached that level. I think there should be boundaries, even with kissing. ❀

What Say You?

1) What standards have you set for yourself in order to honor the Lord with your body (see 1 Corinthians 6:18-20)?

2) Do you know someone who has suffered a consequence of sexual sin?

3) Name three payoffs that result from obeying God's command for sexual purity.

Beauty Secrets

Check it out:
1 Peter 3:3-4

Do you like to pamper yourself? I sure do! Approximately once a month, usually on a Sunday afternoon, I indulge in a head-to-toe buff and polish that takes several hours to accomplish. Although it's time-consuming, I consider it worthwhile because it makes me feel superclean and refreshed, like I've been to a spa!

If you're interested, here's a description of what my regimen entails:

- Soak in a bubble bath for thirty minutes, followed by skin exfoliation. (I light candles and turn on relaxing music for a true spa effect.)
- Remove unwanted facial and body hair with tweezers and hair removal cream.
- Moisturize body.
- Steam face, then use exfoliation scrub and facial moisturizer.
- Groom eyebrows (I get them waxed professionally once a month).

- Manicure fingernails.
- Give toenails a pedicure.
- Bleach teeth.
- Wash hair.

Voilà! I feel like a new person afterward. Not only is my home spa treatment rejuvenating, it's also a free service because I do it myself.

For the rest of the month, I don't spend much time on maintenance—just a few tweaks here and there to keep myself up. (For example, I exfoliate my face whenever needed, not just once a month.)

I do these things not only to feel great but also to enhance my appearance. I realized a long time ago I'm never going to look like a supermodel or a Miss America contestant. I'm five foot seven, I have very fair skin, and I'm medium boned. That's the way God made me. If I spent hours thinking about how much I wanted to look like singer Carrie Underwood or supermodel Gisele Bündchen, I'd be wasting time. However, by putting a little effort into the person I see in the mirror, I'm enhancing what God gave me to work with: my *own* attributes.

It's sad that so many girls (and guys, for that matter) are unhappy in their skin. They compare themselves to the most gorgeous models and actors, and buy into messages from the culture that say they don't measure up. I'll admit I've been trapped by this way of thinking too, and it has caused me unnecessary grief. But I'm glad I've come to a place of greater acceptance about how God, who created me in His own image, designed my frame.

Have you arrived at that place of contentment too, or are you wishing you looked like someone else? If you're comparing yourself to other people, I can tell you it's futile and emotionally unhealthy to engage in that way of thinking. It will only bring you pain.

I'm reminded of a quote I've always liked: "Be yourself. Everyone else is taken." In other words, you need to find peace with who you are, but I'm going to take it a step further: you need to find peace with who you are *in the Lord* and appreciate the way He uniquely designed you—your hair, the color of your eyes, your face, your legs, and even your buns and hips. As one of my girlfriends said one time with a smile on her face, "Hey, I've got *great* birthing hips!" If you don't like a certain feature, that's okay. Downplay it. But accept yourself as God made you. Don't feel short-changed because you don't resemble some celebrity who has most likely been touched up, surgically enhanced, and given numerous makeovers and hair extension treatments. (Then, after all that, she steps into the glare of public scrutiny and hopes people will think she was born beautiful.)

While we're on the subject, here's a good example of how beauty is not always as it seems. My friend Dave worked with TV star Pamela Anderson on the set of her television series, and he told me it took her two hours to look like "Pam." He said that when she arrived at the studio each day, she didn't match the fierce image she portrays to the public—not even close! But after getting "Pammed out" by her hair and makeup artists, she had a completely different look.

Most of us are aware of the hours that go into making celebs look hot, but we still get enticed by the flawless images we see.

What female star do you consider drop-dead gorgeous? Is there someone who fits your ideal of physical perfection?

Well, forgive me for blowing out your candle, so to speak, but consider this morbid reality: that girl or woman you think is so breathtaking will no longer be on this planet in approximately eighty years or less, and she will have moved beyond her peak of beauty long before that. If you find that depressing, I apologize, but that's the dead-honest truth. Pardon the pun.

Even the Bible mentions some lovely women, like Sarah (see Genesis 12:11), Rebekah (see Genesis 24:16), Rachel (see Genesis 29:17), Abigail (see 1 Samuel 25:3), Esther (see Esther 2:7), and Job's daughters (see Job 42:15). Their beauty didn't last forever either. Those biblical babes grew old and died, just like everyone else.

Think of the gorgeous Hollywood starlets from the past—Greta Garbo, Sophia Loren, Marilyn Monroe, Lana Turner, Audrey Hepburn. Where are they now? Their bodies are either old or cold (i.e., dead). As beautiful as they were—and they all were considered very sexy and glamorous in their prime—their beauty didn't last. All that remains of their ravishing good looks is what you see on film or in print.

I remember going to the Broadway musical *Sunset Boulevard* with my parents years ago. It's a sad story of an aging actress who is unable to accept that the beauty and fame she once possessed is gone, and she tries desperately to deny what time has done to her. This woman believes the lie that her worth as a human being is dependent on youth and glamour, and when it is gone, she becomes a tragic old has-been.

What can we learn from this? I'll let the wisdom in the book of Proverbs do the talking: "Charm is deceptive, and beauty is fleeting; but a woman who fears the LORD is to be praised" (Proverbs 31:30).

This passage emphasizes that physical attractiveness is temporary and that it's far more important to invest your time in what is eternal: your relationship with God! By reading your Bible, communicating with the Lord through prayer, and involving yourself in some kind of ministry or service, you can acquire the kind of *inner* beauty that is fade-resistant.

Does this mean you should feel guilty for spending time on yourself physically (or in my case, spending an afternoon at my "home spa")? No. The Lord understands your need to feel attractive, but He wants you to keep it in perspective. Your greatest priority should be your relationship with Him—not obsessing over your appearance or dwelling on female celebrities you wish you could resemble.

The popular culture creates a fantasy world of glamour, exhilarating sex, perpetual youth, and unimaginable happiness. It is a fraud! The gorgeous celebrities we idolize experience the same insecurities and depressing moments that plague the rest of us. So before you compare yourself negatively to the best and the brightest among them, take a moment to thank the Lord for His love and His perfect plan for your life. He created you for a purpose, and His purpose is not dependent on your age or physical limitations.

In 1 Samuel 16:7, we learn, "The LORD does not look at the things man looks at. Man looks at the outward appearance, but the LORD looks at the heart."

Suzanne Woods Fisher wrote this thought-provoking statement about the heart in a *Today's Christian Woman* article entitled "What I'm Learning about . . . Physical Appearance":

> The heart—known in the Hebrew language as the inner person, the seat of thought and emotion, [is]

the decision maker, the responder to God's calling. Unlike our exterior genetic packaging, the heart's condition is within our control. God looks at the inner person when He sees us. Our outside packaging is temporal window dressing; our heart is destined for eternity.

When God looks at *your* heart, does He see a beautiful inner person, destined for eternity? The answer is within your control.

LET'S TALK ABOUT BEAUTY

ALYSON THOMAS (student, age 16): I think it's important for female friends to compliment and build each other up. Guys don't always give us positive reinforcement, yet we wonder what they think of us and if they like how we look. Our girlfriends can help in that way. Recently my friend was styling my hair for the prom, and she told me I looked beautiful. That was the first time anyone said that to me, and it meant so much!

MARY SPAGNOLA (student, age 16): We are our own toughest critics when it comes to our bodies and our appearance. I've noticed that when my friends feel self-conscious about their flaws, they draw attention to them, and quite often I hadn't noticed until they pointed them out. For example, a friend might say, "I have a huge zit on my face," and I'll look at her and ask, "Where?" So we need to remember that other people aren't as hard on us as we are on ourselves.

SARAH UTTERBACK (student, age 16): I used to be more image conscious. I would see an advertisement and think,

I gotta look like that—I need to buy that makeup or hair care product. But lately I've been working on feeling more comfortable with who I am. If I go to school without straightening my hair and just let it dry naturally, friends will say, "Your hair looks so good today!" It's surprising to me that they think my hair looks nice when I haven't done anything to try to improve it. I've realized that the way God created my hair is better than what I try to do to change it.

PASTOR AUSTIN DUNCAN (youth minister): The majority of teen girl conversations revolve around the three Bs—buddies, bodies, and boys. I encourage girls to add a fourth B to those topics—the Bible—and to ask themselves what God's Word has to say about true beauty, their bodies, and their appearance. When girls study the Bible, they find deep fulfillment in discovering what it means to be a woman of God.

MRS. KRISTIN SALLADIN (home educators co-op director): I like to watch old black-and-white movies, and sometimes I'll look up biographies of the beautiful actresses from the past. I've been saddened to learn that most of their lives did not end well. I'm reminded that physical attractiveness in and of itself doesn't amount to much.

DUSTY SANDERSON (student, age 17): A lot of girls at my school try to turn situations to their advantage and control others. I think that's repulsive. To me, an attractive girl is someone who's super nice and respectful, with a spirit of humility. It's not how she looks or dresses that ultimately makes her an attractive person; it's her character qualities.

MARIN JOHNSEN (student, age 15): Society tells us that beauty is having symmetrical facial features and a great *body, but what we look like on the outside doesn't have anything to do with real beauty. God says that real beauty comes from the heart.*

BECCA YOUNKMAN (student, age 17): *You'll notice someone's outward appearance first, but it's what's on the inside that makes a person attractive or not. You might think a girl isn't very pretty at first glance, but when you get to know her, you think,* She really has authentic beauty. *The opposite is true too. A lot of people are beautiful on the outside, and then you find out they're nasty and stuck-up.*

PASTOR AUSTIN DUNCAN (youth minister): *Proverbs 11:22 says, "Like a gold ring in a pig's snout is a beautiful woman who shows no discretion." I desire for girls to understand what it means to have sound judgment, which is the definition of discernment. The book of Proverbs is filled with wisdom for girls on how to be a godly woman, including an entire chapter that's devoted to that topic [Proverbs 31].*

What do you think about makeup?

MARIN JOHNSEN (student, age 15): *It bugs me when girls cake on foundation so their face looks a different color from their neck. I've made the mistake of putting on too much foundation too, but I try to extend it down my neck and blend it in.*

ELISSA MASON (student, age 14): *My brother makes comments like, "That girl would be prettier if she'd take off some makeup." I've also heard tons of guys at school say the same thing. They'll say, "She wears too much makeup, and it looks terrible." I think some girls try too hard with makeup. They need to tone it down.*

JENNA SALLADIN *(student, age 17):* A guy told me that a girl shouldn't look shockingly different when she steps out of a swimming pool after her makeup has worn off. When I put my makeup on, I try to make sure I still look like myself.

MRS. KRISTIN SALLADIN *(home educators co-op director):* Makeup has its place. As my pastor said one time, "If the barn needs painting, paint it!"

Describe someone you think is beautiful.

BECCA YOUNKMAN *(student, age 17):* I have a friend who dresses modestly and doesn't wear much makeup. She never talks negatively about people, and she's forgiving when they make mistakes. I admire her beautiful heart.

ELISSA MASON *(student, age 14):* One of my friends may never be America's next top model, but she's a sweet person, and her love for the Lord is contagious. She walks around giving people hugs and encouraging them. She is the essence of true beauty.

PAUL HONTZ *(student, age 19):* I have a friend named Carleigh who I think is beautiful. She is strong in her Christian walk, and the way she treats everyone is very attractive to me.

CHRISTIAN TURNER *(student, age 16):* There's a girl at my school I would say is beautiful. She's very self-assured in her relationship with Christ, and she doesn't try to find her self-worth in what others think of her. She also believes that some things are nonnegotiable, such as abstinence, and she's not ashamed to let people know. I admire that.

What Say You?

1) What are some physical features that you like about yourself?

2) Are you content with the way God made you, or have you been guilty of wishing that you looked like someone else? What attitude does the Lord want you to have regarding your appearance?

3) Name three ways you can acquire inner beauty (the fade-resistant kind).

4) What should be your greatest priority?

Zip Up and Button Down

Check it out:

1 Corinthians 6:19-20

Recently I saw a film that featured a couple going on a date. The woman's dress was so revealing that I was actually embarrassed for her, even though she was only a fictitious character in a story line. I thought to myself, *How can a woman expect to be taken seriously in a getup like that?*

When you're around guys, do you dress in a way that encourages respect? Do you prefer that they actually *listen* to your views on global warming instead of thinking about the two inches of cleavage you're sporting? If you're wearing clothes that are too tight, too short, or too low, guys are going to be distracted by what you're showcasing. They might even assume you're unintelligent or sexually promiscuous. By dressing more modestly, you'll give them the opportunity to notice that you have a brain and a personality!

I'm reminded of what I heard one guy say: "We might like it when a girl dresses sexy, but we don't respect her for it." Very insightful! Sometimes I think of that statement when I see a girl in a micromini or a low-cut top. I wish she understood that her skimpy little number isn't drawing the kind of admiration she truly desires.

And what about the guys she's flaunting herself in front of? Doesn't she have a responsibility to help them control their sexual thoughts? Jesus said in Matthew 5 that any man who even *looks* at a woman lustfully has already committed the sin of adultery with her in his heart.

Girls, if you only knew how much Christian guys struggle with lust of the eyes and lust of the flesh. It's an ongoing battle! Because of that, you have a spiritual obligation to not add to their dilemma.

Not long ago I was in line at the post office where a woman standing at the counter was wearing a very tight, low-cut dress. The man in front of me could not take his eyes off her and was ogling her up and down. I think I had a pretty good read of what was going through his mind!

You are called to a higher standard than to dress in a way that would cause a man to stumble (see 1 Corinthians 10:32). As a woman of God, you need to be mindful of whether or not your choice of attire is appropriate.

There's a greater issue here that goes beyond protecting your brothers in Christ. It centers on the fact that your body belongs to the Lord (see 1 Corinthians 6:19-20). Because of that, how you dress your body should honor Him.

Let me ask you a question: When you get up in the morning and thumb through your closet to figure out what to wear, do you realize that your decision is spiritual? It is! Your wardrobe should be pleasing to the Lord. If you're unsure if an outfit is acceptable, just ask Him. I've done that before, and He has brought Scripture verses to my mind that provided me with insight. One verse in particular was 1 Corinthians 10:31: "Whether you eat or drink or whatever you do, do it all for the glory of God." I realized that the "whatever you do" is relevant even for my clothing selections.

So are you bumming at the thought of wearing high-neck shirts and ankle-length skirts the rest of your life? Think again! You can wear clothes that are honoring to the Lord and still fashionable and fun! You can look great without relying on plunging necklines, tight Lycra tops, microminis, and ultra-low-rise jeans that reveal thong underwear when you bend down to pick something off the floor.

The next time you're at church or school, check out the various outfits the girls are wearing. Look for figure-flattering clothes that don't show too much skin. You might even get some ideas for your own wardrobe. Just the other day I saw a girl at the movie rental store wearing a cute pair of plum-colored corduroys. I got up the nerve to ask her where she bought them, and she was happy to tell me, mentioning that they came in lots of other colors. I just may need to make a pit stop at the store and try on a pair or two. Whether your personal style is classic, trendy, funky, or flashy, you can put together plenty of head-turning options that stay within spiritual limits. When in doubt, you can always fall back on your most reliable selection: your favorite jeans and a cute top or T-shirt. It's appropriate for any casual setting, and guys will go for that look every time! In fact, one guy told me that a nice-fitting pair of jeans was his hands-down favorite style of clothing on a girl.

Have some fashion fun, but remember to dress modestly. As a Christian, you have a responsibility to the Lord, to the male species, and to yourself to develop some standards of decency. Clothes that shout, "Sex!" give the wrong message, so zip up and button down.

LET'S TALK ABOUT CLOTHES

REBECCA YOUNG (student, age 16): My mom told me that if a girl dresses immodestly, she's showing disrespect for guys—it's like the girl is telling them that they're shallow and they only care about looking at her body.

MARY SPAGNOLA (student, age 16): I think guys tend to treat a girl based upon how she's dressed. If she dresses sexy, then they treat her as an object. But if she dresses with respect for herself, then guys are more likely to respond to her with respect.

SARAH UTTERBACK (student, age 16): When my former boyfriend and I were dating, he told me that the first time he started liking me was at our junior retreat, and what I was wearing that day was just a pair of jeans and a sweatshirt.

ALYSON THOMAS (student, age 16): When it comes to necklines, my rule is this: If I can see my "girls," then I shouldn't be wearin' the top! So if I look down and notice that I'm revealing something, then I won't wear that article of clothing anymore. I think you can wear outfits that make you feel beautiful even though you're completely covered. When people look at you, they won't be thinking about what part of your body you're exposing—they'll just be thinking how pretty you are.

MATT GODSHALL (student, age 14): Obviously a girl doesn't need to cover herself up with gigantic jackets to be modest, but before going out, she should look in the mirror and analyze how much skin she's showing.

ERIN DIEFENBACH (student, age 17): I dress much more

conservatively than the other girls at my school. I want to be Christlike and honor the guys as well as myself by how I dress. I am God's temple and He resides in me, so I need to represent Him well. One question that I ask myself occasionally is, If I went to dinner with God, would I wear what I have on right now?

SAMANTHA BOWSER (student, age 17): I went to a school dance with a guy friend recently and noticed two girls wearing short, strapless minidresses. You could see everything! My date, Kyle, dropped his jaw when he saw them, and I jokingly closed his mouth and made a comment about how he couldn't take his eyes off of them. Kyle replied, "No, Samantha, you don't understand. Those girls caught my attention, but I would never want to be with a girl who dresses like that. It's unattractive and degrading."

MR. AUSTIN SEFTON (youth leader): It's important for girls to realize how much teen guys struggle sexually and what goes through their minds at a time when so many hormones are fluctuating. Yes, Christian guys have a relationship with Christ and have the Spirit to guide them, but because they're not perfect, they can still fail. The number one sin for most guys is lust of the eyes, so it's easy for them to stumble by looking at a woman who's dressed inappropriately. A girl can help her brothers in Christ by dressing modestly. The culture communicates that to be attractive you need to show skin and advertise yourself, but as a Christian young woman, you're not part of that game. Showing skin to try to attract the hottest guy shouldn't be your ambition—you're called to a higher standard.

GUYS ONLY: *What do you think about girls who dress immodestly?*

DUSTY SANDERSON (student, age 17): Obviously if a girl dresses sexy, I'm going to notice her, but the truth is, it drives me away. It doesn't motivate me to want to approach her, talk to her, or be her friend. Dressing that way gives a message that the girl doesn't have high standards. Sure, she's going to attract attention, but it's not going to come from the kind of guys she wants. If she dresses "bad," she's going to attract "bad." A Christian girl can rely on her personality and her walk with the Lord to get attention, which are greater sources of attractiveness.

JONATHAN YOUNKMAN (student, age 15): If a girl wears a revealing outfit, it's like she's saying, "Hey, I'm here! Look at me! I want more attention than I usually get!"

BEN TRAPP (student, age 15): Some girls feel a need to show their belly-button ring, and I'm thinking, No, you don't! When a girl dresses sexy, it makes me think, Wow, you are not my type! Why do some girls stoop to that level to get guys to notice them? I'm more impressed when I see girls do random acts of kindness.

CHRISTIAN TURNER (student, age 16): Girls who dress immodestly take away the mystery, and a lot of guys (myself included) prefer mystery.

DAVID STRUM (student, age 15): A guy's head is on a swivel. God made us visually oriented, so that's the way we are. For instance, I'll be talking to a guy friend at school, and his head will whip to the side. I'll turn around and see a scantily clad girl. Then I'll turn back to my friend and say, "Dude, I'm *talking to you—stop looking at her!"* I don't think girls realize the kind of pressure they put guys under by dressing immodestly. Honestly, I feel sorry for girls who think they have to dress that way to get attention. A lot of girls would be just as pretty in long sleeves and jeans, so why wear revealing clothes if it's not necessary?

MATT GODSHALL (student, age 14): It's cool if girls want to look pretty, but occasionally I'll see clothing at church that I don't think is appropriate. I do my best not to check girls out because I don't want to look at them lustfully. When I do catch myself checking a girl out, I immediately look away and mumble these words: "Jesus Christ, Son of God, have mercy on me!" I learned that phrase at a retreat, and it helps to say it because I associate checking out a girl with the need to ask for forgiveness. My purity standard is high, so I would appreciate it if girls would do their part to help me maintain that. I don't think a guy's battle with lust is something he can ever say he's done with. It's ongoing.

GUYS ONLY: *What styles of girls' clothing do you like?*

DUSTY SANDERSON (student, age 17): I like it when girls wear athletic warm-up clothes, such as hoodies and sweatpants. My sister is a good example of someone who dresses fashionably and modestly. She wears the latest style of jeans, and skirts with hem lengths just above the knee.

JON SALLADIN (student, age 15): I love it when girls wear turtleneck sweaters in the winter months.

DAVID STRUM (student, age 15): Jeans are always a good choice. If she wears a V-neck shirt, the "V" shouldn't go down to her stomach!

CHRISTIAN TURNER *(student, age 16):* I prefer sundresses with shoulder straps and appropriate necklines.

JONATHAN YOUNKMAN *(student, age 15):* A girl can attract attention while being fully clothed. If she wears a nice top and jeans, she can look really pretty. But the shirt shouldn't be tight. If she wants to wear a low-cut shirt, then she can put a T-shirt on underneath.

PAUL HONTZ *(student, age 19):* I think any trendy style can be pulled off in modest fashion.

Girls only: What styles of clothing do you like to wear?

ELISSA MASON *(student, age 14):* I like to wear trendy jeans and tanks. I can find tanks for only about five bucks, and I wear sweaters over them and cute necklaces.

JENNA SALLADIN *(student, age 17):* I like dresses and sundresses. If I need to, I wear tanks underneath.

MARIN JOHNSEN *(student, age 15):* I like to layer my clothes, and I find a lot of cute styles for decent prices. ✿

What Say You?

1) What clothing styles do you like that honoring to the Lord?

2) What thoughts run through your mind when you see a girl wearing an inappropriate outfit?

3) As a Christian, to whom do you have a responsibility in regard to your clothing selections? (Hint: There's more than one source.)

Weight a Minute!

Check it out:

Romans 12:2

Is it just me, or are you equally fed up with the pressure to be superthin? I mean, it seems like every company is trying to sell us diet tablets, fat-burning techniques, exercise equipment, or weight-loss shakes! And what really grates on my nerves are the messages, often nonverbal, that accompany the products. How many ads and infomercials have you seen that feature a gorgeous girl in a bikini, stepping out of a swimming pool, who appears to have the world at her command? She has every guy's full attention, and she's so thrilled with her hot bod that she couldn't switch off her one-thousand-watt smile if she tried. The company's message is clear: buy our products, and you will be just as sexy as she is! So you cave in and purchase the diet pills or whatever, only to find out that even if you lose weight, the cute guys still aren't pounding down your door. Reality stinks, doesn't it?

Hey, I'm not minimizing the fact that being in shape feels fantastic. It's also very healthy! But what annoys me is the constant harassment by the diet and fitness companies to make us believe we don't measure up (literally). All in the name of trying to make a buck!

It's not just these manufacturers that contribute to our struggle with self-acceptance. Many experts believe the media and entertainment industries are also responsible because they pummel us with images of bodily perfection. Supermodels, Hollywood divas, celebrity babes and hunks —the effect on people is profound, not only in this country, but around the world!

This was illustrated dramatically when American satellite television was first introduced in the South Pacific in the early 1990s. Suddenly, girls on the island of Fiji were saturated with images of gorgeous, stick-figured Hollywood actresses who starred on hit shows. Four years later, a survey was conducted with sixty-five of these young Fiji women to reveal how their attitudes had been shaped (or as I see it, warped) by their viewing experience. The results were astounding! Almost immediately upon seeing the beautiful starlets on TV, the girls in Fiji began to dress and style their hair like American actresses. Their eating habits also dramatically changed. Those who watched TV three times per week were 50 percent more likely to perceive themselves as too fat than those who watched less often. And more than 62 percent of the girls had attempted to diet sometime during the past month!

As you might expect, girls here at home took it to a whole new level. A study in the early 1990s revealed that 80 percent of fourth-grade girls had attempted to diet because they perceived themselves as fat. Eighty percent! The main reason for this, the study concluded, is that today's youth are immersed in a culture where messages about dieting and being thin are everywhere. In fact, the fear of becoming fat is so threatening that even those who are an average weight are terrified of putting on pounds. Some of these slim people already think they're fat!

My friend Kelly fell prey to this mind-set. She's an average weight and looks fantastic, but several years ago her mother walked into Kelly's room and found her lying on her bed with tears in her eyes. When asked what was wrong, she replied, "Mom, I'm fat! I need to lose weight. I'm just too fat!" Her mother immediately became suspicious and asked, "Did the Victoria's Secret catalog come today?" Kelly sheepishly admitted that it had. Her mother sighed. "Kelly, those women have been airbrushed and touched up. The images you see in the catalog aren't realistic, and there's no expression of heart and soul." Kelly realized her mom was right and made a decision that day to call the Victoria's Secret company and request that her name be removed from the mailing list. She told her mom she no longer wanted to compare herself to those perfect images.

While we're on the subject, here's something else to consider: a friend told me that she knows the therapist for a few of the Victoria's Secret models, and the therapist described them as being "a mess." He said they were unhappy, stressed, and bulimic. He went on to say, "Believe me when I tell you things are not always as they seem."

If some of the babes featured on the glossy pages of Victoria's Secret aren't flying high with self-acceptance, what message does that send to the rest of us? I'm sure you've figured it out, but I'll make a statement for the record: being skinny and attractive is not the key to happiness and satisfaction!

Then what is? Ah, I'm glad you asked! I bet you think I'm going to say Jesus is the answer, right? Well, He *is* the answer, but not for the purpose of happiness and satisfaction. Don't allow anyone to tell you that being a follower of Christ is your ticket to euphoria. Jesus assured us in John 16:33, "In this world you will have trouble." No, being a Christian isn't a guarantee of happiness, but it *is* the pathway to contentment if you'll strive for it. The apostle Paul stated in Philippians 4:11-13: "I have learned to be content whatever the circumstances. I know what it is to be in need, and I know what it is to have plenty. I have learned the secret of being content in any and every situation, whether well fed or hungry, whether living in plenty or in want. I can do everything through him who gives me strength."

Becoming content with your body is part of the Philippians 4:11-13 equation. That doesn't mean you shouldn't exercise or watch what you eat, but it *does* free you to accept yourself at a healthy weight.

I remember the "Happy to Be Me" doll that came out a while back. This toy was the alternative to Barbie, with hips, thighs, and a more realistic waistline. This doll wasn't designed to appear overweight—just average. Barbie, on the other hand, has a bustline three times the size of her waist! Years ago, my dad used to joke that the only flaw on Barbie is the stamp on her buns that reads, "Made in China."

Shouldn't we all adopt a "happy to be me" philosophy, accepting our bodies the way God made them and not conforming to the propaganda society lays on us?

Here's what the Bible has to say on the subject: "Do not conform any longer to the pattern of this world, but be transformed by the renewing of your mind" (Romans 12:2).

We can begin renewing our minds by taking our focus off the supermodels and putting it on our *role model*,

Jesus Christ! He's our only answer for true peace and contentment.

LET'S TALK ABOUT BODY IMAGE

SAMANTHA BOWSER (student, age 17): I don't like words like fat, skinny, or overweight. God made people of all different shapes and sizes, and I think we should be okay with that.

FRANKIE OGAZ (student, age 16): I love to play softball, and if I wasn't thick and sturdy, I wouldn't have the same level of strength. God made me the way I am for a reason, and I choose to love myself as He created me.

Guys only: A lot of girls think they need to be superthin to be considered attractive. What do you think?

DAVID STRUM (student, age 15): It doesn't matter to me if a girl eats a lot, as long as she's healthy. I know a girl who plays soccer and eats a ton of food, but she's not overweight—she looks great. So if a girl can eat a lot and still look healthy, I say more power to her!

DUSTY SANDERSON (student, age 17): I like it when a girl respects her body by keeping it healthy—not overly skinny or overly big, but in good shape. When I go someplace for lunch or dinner with a girl, I like for her to enjoy her food and not pick at her plate. I don't like it when she makes comments like, "Oh, I already ate" or "I don't want to eat very much." I'm thinking, Come on, it's okay to eat!

DAVID STRUM (student, age 15): If a guy thinks you have to be skinny to be attractive, then he's not worth your time.

MATT GODSHALL *(student, age 14): Society tells us what we should look like, but those messages aren't half as intense for guys as they are for girls. For me personally, a girl's body doesn't matter as much as who she is as a person.*

JON SALLADIN *(student, age 15): I eat a lot, so I think it's attractive if a girl has a hearty appetite—as long as she's not obese.*

JONATHAN YOUNKMAN *(student, age 15): I like to see a girl eat a nice-sized portion of food. She doesn't need to be superthin for me to find her attractive. As long as she looks healthy, she'll get my attention.* ❁

What Say You?

1) Do you often compare yourself to flawless images you see in advertisements and throughout the entertainment industry? If so, how does that make you feel?

2) What do you think it means to learn to be content in every circumstance (see Philippians 4:11-13)? How does that relate to accepting your body?

3) Do you like what you see in the mirror? If not, pray and ask God to help you perceive yourself the same way that He does: "fearfully and wonderfully made" (Psalm 139:14).

Balancing the Scale

Check it out:

1 Corinthians 10:31

Not long ago my parents and I went out to dinner with a good friend. During the meal, he talked about the struggle his seventeen-year-old daughter, Caitlin, had with bulimia (an eating disorder where a person binges on food and then forces herself to vomit). He said that his family had found out about her bulimia just one month earlier, and they were stunned and deeply grieved. My parents and I sympathized with our friend and assured him that we would be praying for his family, and especially for Caitlin.

Later, as I began to write this chapter on the topic of eating disorders, the Lord seemed to encourage me to contact Caitlin and ask if she would feel comfortable sharing her story. I called her, and she was kind and very receptive to my request.

Before we started the interview, I prayed on the phone and asked God to bless our conversation and use Caitlin to help other girls who are controlled by an eating disorder. I also asked the Lord to continue to bring healing and restoration to her as she attempted to overcome her addiction.

The following conversation is what transpired after that:

$\mathcal{D}$anae: Caitlin, let me start by asking if there's something specific that you would like to share about your struggle with bulimia.

CAITLIN: Well, as far as my health is concerned, bingeing and purging hasn't been worth all the pain and trouble I've gone through to stay thin. I've discovered there are healthier ways to control my weight.

$\mathcal{D}$anae: I'm so glad you've come to that realization. In what ways has bulimia affected your health?

CAITLIN: Even though I'm still involved with sports, there are a lot of things I can't do anymore without feeling dizzy—even simple things like styling my hair and putting on makeup. I also feel shaky at times, and I've started having migraine headaches. My hands have become very weak too. I've seen a neurologist twice, and I've had two MRIs [magnetic resonance imaging, a type of X-ray scan]. The doctor discovered that my stomach cannot absorb my body's own B_{12} energy anymore, so I've had to get B_{12} shots. Bulimia has affected me not only physically but emotionally. I've become "closed off" to others—like, I never cry, and I'm more secretive.

$\mathcal{D}$anae: I'm very sorry to hear about your pain. Have you stopped bingeing and purging now?

CAITLIN: Yes. I haven't done it for two months. I didn't want to give it up, really, because I kept thinking, I'll get fat! I'll get fat! but I knew I had to stop. I didn't want to keep buying into Satan's lies.

$\mathcal{D}$anae: Do you feel stronger now than you did two months ago, when you first quit?

CAITLIN: Oh yeah. I actually stopped purging before I told anyone. There was an older lady—a friend of my family's—who felt like God had laid me on her heart, and she asked me on three separate occasions if I was doing okay. The first two times I said I was fine and everything was great, but I was actually really depressed. When she asked me the third time, I finally told her the truth. At that point I knew I needed to tell my parents too.

Danae: **How did they react?**

CAITLIN: They were very concerned. My dad was a little confused because I don't think it's easy for men to understand the body issues that women struggle with, but he was supportive. Both my parents responded in love, and they were there for me when I needed them.

Danae: **I'm so glad to hear that. Your dad mentioned that you went to see a counselor. Did that help?**

CAITLIN: Yes. I've had one session so far, and my mom suggested today that I call the counselor and set up another appointment. I'm going to do that.

Danae: **Good idea! That's really important in your recovery. Caitlin, let's back up for a moment. When did you first begin bingeing and purging?**

CAITLIN: A year and a half ago.

Danae: **Was there something in particular that triggered it?**

CAITLIN: I wanted to live a perfect life and have a perfect body. I wanted to be "the pretty girl" people liked to be around. I also wanted attention from my friends, especially guys. I discovered that when I had a good body, I got a lot of attention, and that gave me positive reinforcement to keep purging. I didn't really start purging to lose weight— I just wanted to stay thin.

𝒟*anae:* **That's interesting, because research confirms what you just said—that behind an eating disorder is a need for acceptance and an overwhelming attempt to control one's life. As Christians, however, we don't need to concern ourselves with trying to micromanage our lives. The Spirit of God is living within us, and He is controlling the details. Caitlin, now that you've stopped bingeing and purging, how have your eating habits changed?**

CAITLIN: I eat small meals and a snack here and there. I also drink lots of liquids, including vitamin water or Gatorade.

𝒟*anae:* **Do you have friends who are battling eating disorders?**

CAITLIN: Yes. I know a few people who have been hospitalized two or three times because of anorexia and bulimia. Eating disorders are so hard on the body! One friend of mine won't admit she has a problem, and I'm watching her dwindle away before my eyes. She's anorexic, and she's down to about 85 pounds. She counts calories to the extreme.

𝒟*anae:* **That is so sad. . . . I will pray for her. What advice would you give to others who are harming their bodies in an effort to be thin?**

CAITLIN: Stop doing it before it gets worse—or it will get worse! It's not worth the pain you will go through. Whatever stage you're in, do whatever is necessary to get control.

Also, look in the mirror, smile, and tell yourself you are beautiful.

Danae: **That's very good advice; God made us in His image, so we** are **beautiful. Another thing I would add is that each of us needs to sink our roots deeper in our relationship with the Lord for our emotional and physical well-being. That's the only way we're going to have a healthy sense of identity and self-confidence. There is nothing else—not beauty, a great body, attention from guys, money, popularity, fame, or fulfilling our dreams— that is going to provide lasting satisfaction. Those things might supply a temporary "fix," but nothing of permanence. Only Jesus can give us what we need to feel fulfilled. And He is so willing.**

CAITLIN: That's very true.

Danae: **Before we finish, let me ask you what you've learned spiritually through your experience. What has the Lord taught you?**

CAITLIN: He's taught me that my beauty is found in Him. "Charm is deceptive, and beauty is fleeting; but a woman who fears the LORD is to be praised" [Proverbs 31:30].

Danae: **That's a great Scripture; we all need to meditate on that. Caitlin, thank you for your time and for being so open and honest in your responses. I will continue to pray for your recovery. I'm certain that God will keep using you to help others who are in that same "dark valley" you've walked through. For now, the Lord needs to get you completely restored, and I believe He will do that.**

CAITLIN: I think He will too. 🏵

What a precious girl! My heart really went out to Caitlin as she shared her painful experience. I just know that God is going to help her triumph.

Do you know someone who is bulimic like Caitlin was, or perhaps suffering from anorexia nervosa like her friend? Have you yourself dealt with these same issues? As you can see after reading Caitlin's story, eating disorders can result in serious physical complications. Bulimia has caused Caitlin to suffer muscular weakness, vitamin deficiencies, and nervous system disturbances. Bulimia can also lead to tooth decay, gum erosion, heart problems, tears in the esophagus, and even death if left untreated. I thank God that Caitlin stopped bingeing and purging before it was too late. She also made the right choice in breaking the silence and talking about her struggle with a friend and with her parents. That was an important step in her healing process.

If you know someone who is battling an eating disorder, don't be afraid to confront that person in a spirit of love and concern. Offer to help and do whatever you can to reach out to your friend. Pray for her, encourage her to talk to a trusted adult, and share this chapter with her. Your efforts might start your friend on the road to recovery.

Most people who have eating disorders don't like to admit they need help because they want to manage their behavior on their own. The fact is that they cannot. As Caitlin said, Satan used her eating disorder to take more and more control of her life. She needed others who cared about her to come alongside her and lend their prayers and support. It's well documented by medical professionals that anorexia and bulimia are too complicated for self-treatment.

I remember reading about an actress who confessed to being anorexic, and she said that one time she ate three slices of an orange and felt so guilty that she immediately ran ten miles. I realized that for her to do something that extreme, she obviously had a major body image problem going on in her head. Her obsession to stay slim (at the risk of her own health) would not be cured simply by waking up one morning and saying to herself, *I'm never going to do that again.*

If you're dealing with an eating disorder, please talk to someone you trust, and ask that person to help you find the right professional(s) to help you. It's essential that you receive a medical checkup to assess your health and that you get nutritional support. You also need spiritual counsel, like Caitlin benefited from, and possibly psychological treatment. In the next chapter I provide you with contact information for a wonderful Christian ministry that specializes in assisting people who have eating disorders or other challenges. You don't have to feel lonely in your struggle—there are those who want to help you, especially your heavenly Father!

The Lord loves you and desires for you to accept your body just as He made you. That doesn't mean He has given you the green light to load up on chili cheese fries and never exercise, but He wants you to have a positive body image and to keep your food intake and exercise plan within healthy limits.

Perhaps your battle isn't with bulimia or anorexia but rather with obesity or maybe just needing to choose more healthful foods instead of fast food and sweets. Whatever your struggle, it isn't too big for the Lord to resolve. Success will not happen overnight, but as you daily spend time in His Word, pray, and surrender your eating habits, along with your fears and struggles, He will help you achieve victory.

"What is impossible with men is possible with God" (Luke 18:27).

LET'S TALK ABOUT EATING DISORDERS

SARAH UTTERBACK (student, age 16): Food is one of my passions—I love to eat, so I can't relate to people who deny themselves that pleasure. I have a friend who lost a ton of weight between sixth and seventh grade, and she lost it so fast that it actually scared me. I don't think she did it in a healthy way. It hurt me to see her abuse her body like that, and I could only imagine how God must have felt because He created her.

MARY SPAGNOLA (student, age 16): I want people to accept me for who I am, not for how I look. Some of the girls at school are obsessed with their appearance and their weight, and I've lost respect for them because of that. For instance, they won't eat anything at lunch— they'll just sit there looking hungry. I wish they would at least eat a snack.

PAUL HONTZ (student, age 19): I think that girls worry too much about their weight. There are definitely guys out there who are interested in various "types."

CHRISTIAN TURNER (student, age 16): Scripturally, we've been entrusted with our bodies and need to take care of them. Our bodies are God's temple [2 Corinthians 6:16], so we're accountable for how we treat His holy dwelling place. One way that we can do that is by accepting our diverse shapes and forms as God created them. ❧

What Say You?

1) What is the root cause of an eating disorder? (Hint: It's not the desire to be skinny.)

2) Can a person who is suffering from anorexia or bulimia cure herself on her own? Why or why not?

3) Do you know someone who is living with an eating disorder? What are some ways you can try to help that person?

4) Name three spiritual things you can do to promote a healthy body image.

Self-Harm and Healing

Check it out:

Psalm 55:22

As heartbreaking as it is to think that anyone would try to deal with her emotions by starving herself or bingeing and purging, a more disturbing behavior is when girls engage in self-harm, such as cutting, carving, or burning their bodies. Maybe you know someone who has done this. It's deeply troubling to envision a person deliberately wounding herself, and yet thousands of girls in the United States engage in this harmful behavior each year.[2] Why? To quote one girl: "[When] I could not find the words, cutting had become the language to describe the pain, communicating everything I felt."[3]

Girls who have anorexia or bulimia are especially vulnerable to self-injury. One study reported that up to half of the girls who injure themselves have eating disorders.[4]

[2] Karen L. Suyemoto and X. Kountz, "Self-Mutilation," *The Prevention Researcher* 7 (2000): 1–4.

[3] Tina Takemoto, "Open Wounds," in *Thinking through the Skin*, ed. Sarah Ahmed and Jackie Stacey, (New York, Routledge, 2001), 125.

[4] Armando R. Favazza, *Bodies under Siege: Self-Mutilation and Body Modification in Culture and Psychiatry*, 2nd ed. (Baltimore: Johns Hopkins University Press, 1996).

I wanted to understand this behavior better (as I'm sure you do), so I spoke with Dr. David Wall, an expert at Remuda Ranch, a Christian-based organization for people with eating disorders.[5]

Danae: Dr. Wall, what is the typical age of girls who harm themselves?

DR. WALL: *Primarily adolescents and college-age, in my experience, but it's getting younger, unfortunately.*

Danae: What causes girls to want to injure themselves?

DR. WALL: *Based upon seeing and interviewing a lot of patients over the years, I believe the primary reason for cutting is to provide a way of dealing with emotions. The girls feel a lot of anger or depression, and cutting themselves enables them to experience temporary relief from emotional pain. For whatever reason, cutting causes their internal pain to become external and therefore provides some relief. Sometimes when a person has gone through a past trauma such as sexual abuse, she will relive the experience in her mind and then injure herself as a way to put an end to those thoughts and bring herself back to reality.*

Danae: Are there other reasons besides past traumas that cause girls to inflict pain on themselves?

DR. WALL: *Yes. Quite often the girls who do this come from homes where they don't feel validated or cared about. Many of them struggle with their sense of self-worth, and they don't consider that God has a plan and purpose for*

---

[5] Dr. David Wall is the corporate director of psychology at Remuda Ranch.

their lives. Also, many have never been taught to release their emotions in a healthy way. They haven't seen it modeled in their families, so they start cutting themselves or acting out in other destructive ways, such as through eating disorders or substance abuse.

Danae: **I've read that when girls injure themselves, it produces endorphins in the body, which gives them a sense of well-being. Would you please explain that?**

DR. WALL: *Whenever we experience any kind of pain, our brain releases an endorphin, which is a natural type of morphine [a numbing drug]. When girls inflict pain on themselves, the brain releases this morphine-type substance, which provides a feeling of euphoria, or pleasure. The pain actually causes a temporary sense of well-being that counterbalances the extreme negative emotions they're experiencing.*

Danae: **What an enormous price to pay for a momentary "high." Do these girls typically conceal their wounds, or do they display them as a cry for help?**

DR. WALL: *Some girls attempt to hide their cutting—it's very personal for them. Others are attention seekers, but again, it's usually because they don't feel cared about. They want to be nurtured, but they don't know how to get those needs met in a healthy way. How much more can a person say, "I'm hurting" than to deliberately injure herself?*

Danae: **I can understand that. What areas of the body are the girls most likely to cut?**

DR. WALL: *Typically their arms and legs, but with eating disorder patients we often see girls who have cut the areas of their bodies that they're most disgusted with, such as* their abdomens or thighs. It's a way of expressing anger and hatred toward their bodies.

𝒟anae: That's so sad. Can this behavior develop into an addiction?

DR. WALL: Yes, it can become an addiction or a primary way of coping. Some girls have told us that they've tried cutting and discovered they didn't like it because it hurt. Others became addicted, and once that pattern is established they almost certainly need outside help. They cannot deal with the problem on their own. ❀

If you are living with an eating disorder or with a tendency to self-harm, let me encourage you to call Remuda Ranch at 1-800-445-1900. A friendly staff member will be happy to answer your questions and possibly help you find a specialist in your area. Your call will be kept strictly confidential. If you'd prefer to check out their Web site first, visit http://www.remudaranch.com. Take the necessary steps to get yourself healthy and well. As the organization's slogan says, "Find hope . . . begin healing . . . embrace life."

Marion C. Eberly, a registered nurse at Remuda Ranch, wrote an outstanding article on the topic of self-injurious behavior in which she correlated this modern-day epidemic to a similar trend in biblical times. You may have read about how the prophets of the false god Baal mutilated their bodies by carving and cutting their skin (see 1 Kings 18:28). Eberly explains that their cutting was similar to what self-injurers do today, except for one thing. She writes, "Their [the prophets of Baal] motivation was not to avoid a painful memory or to reject themselves in some way. Their self-injurious acts were done as a ritual sacrifice to a god named Baal. They believed that if they could show this god devotion by imposing severe physical suffering upon themselves they would be seen as worthy."

Did Baal respond? No. But Jehovah (God) did. He sent fire from heaven that burned up God's prophet Elijah's sacrificed bull, altar stones, and wood, and even dried up the trough of water surrounding the altar. Immediately the bleeding Baal worshipers declared that the Lord, not Baal, was God (1 Kings 18:16-39). Eberly says that just as the prophets of Baal lost trust in their own god, people who self-harm often feel abandoned and have lost trust in others. Their response to the repetitive theme of being betrayed by those they trust is to repeat the injury, she says. The self-harm is part of their search for meaning and identity. All the while they're searching for someone to believe in or someone to believe in *them* and to help them "control their inner chaos." So who can really help? Who will believe in those girls?

Ms. Eberly gives the solution: "From a biblical viewpoint, God already believes in them and they belong to Him. He sent His Son, Jesus Christ, to die for them. Jesus gave His life for theirs, sacrificing all He was and all He had. Hebrews 9:11-12 tells us that once for all time Jesus offered His own blood as a sacrifice for our sins, and He secured our salvation with it. He did this so we might have peace, identity, and a secure future through eternal life."[6]

Many who self-harm are searching not only for relief from emotional turmoil but also for meaning and purpose. What they discover in a relationship with Jesus Christ is

---

[6] "Understanding Self-Injurious Behavior in Eating Disorders," *The Remuda Review* 4 (Summer 2005).

a way to get those needs met, and so much more! He loves them unconditionally and has a plan for their lives.

As Ms. Eberly explained so eloquently, "Those who are suffering with self-injury need to have a new tool to put in their hands to replace the razor blades and matches. The Word of God is meant to be that tool which renews our minds, restores our emotions, establishes our identity, and guides our decisions for life."[7]

The Lord knows our thoughts and understands every detail of our deep hurts and sorrows. When those who are suffering give their heartaches to God, "He heals the broken-hearted and binds up their wounds" (Psalm 147:3).

LET'S TALK ABOUT CUTTING

ERIN DIEFENBACH *(student, age 17): I know a girl who is so sweet—she's soft-spoken and complimentary—but she is absolutely covered in scars from cutting. She has scars on her arms, her legs, and even on her back because she has a "cutting buddy." It breaks my heart, and I feel so helpless. I pray for her, and I try to encourage her by saying, "I love you" and "You're beautiful."*

ALYSON THOMAS *(student, age 16): Nothing and nobody should be able to hurt you to the point of making you want to hurt yourself.*

MARY SPAGNOLA *(student, age 16): People I know who have cut themselves wish they had never started because it's addicting and it's hard to stop. If you know someone who is cutting, make sure the person knows you love her and that*

---

[7] Ibid.

she can come to you to talk. That's what I've tried to do for my own friends.

SARAH UTTERBACK *(student, age 16): I watched a movie about a girl whose mom was overly obsessive and her dad was struggling with work issues. Nobody understood her, and she tried to express herself through her artistic abilities without any success. She ended up cutting her body so she could see the pain instead of just feeling it. Cutting was her way to express her emotions. Obviously, that's not the right solution. I believe that prayer can release more emotions than cutting ever could. You should unload all your pain on God and not on your body.* ❀

What Say You?

1) What causes someone to want to injure herself?

2) There is only one way to obtain peace, identity, and a life that holds meaning. What is it?

3) Do you know someone who is addicted to cutting? What are some ways you can reach out to that person this week?

4) Do you believe that God can help someone overcome an addiction, no matter how severe? If you're unsure, remember Christ's promise in Luke 18:27: "What is impossible with men is possible with God."

Our Refuge and Strength

Check it out:

Psalm 56:3-4

When my brother, Ryan, was little, he frequently asked Mom to read the poem "Afraid of the Dark" by Shel Silverstein. In the poem, a young boy named Reginald describes all the things he does before bed to avoid the darkness, such as requesting three bedtime stories, saying several prayers, and making two trips to the bathroom. He also insists on hugging his teddy, rubbing his blanket, and sucking his "thumbie." The poem ends with Reginald saying once more that he's afraid of the dark and pleading, "Do not close this book on me." At that point, my mom would always slam the book shut, which would make Ryan giggle.

Maybe you're not afraid of the dark like Reginald Clark, but is there something else that frightens you (such as being made fun of by classmates, getting into an accident, having your parents divorce, or even losing someone you love)? Now for the tougher question: do you trust God to take care of you if your fear becomes reality? That's a disturbing thought, I know, but worth contemplating.

I'll admit I am still learning to trust the Lord when scary

times come my way. I'm better at it now than I used to be, but finding peace in the midst of a storm is something I'm still working on. What helps is to remember other times when the Lord has carried me through "dark valleys." His presence has given me courage to deal with anxieties that threatened to overwhelm me. As the psalmist wrote in Psalm 77:11-12: "I will remember the deeds of the LORD; yes, I will remember your miracles of long ago. I will meditate on all your works and consider all your mighty deeds."

I witnessed a confirmation of that comforting Scripture in my life earlier this year. It began when my sweet grandmother, "Gram," as I called her, went home to be with Jesus. She had lived a long life, but after ninety-seven years, the Lord gently ushered her soul into eternity. It happened without warning or preparation, and it left me shaken.

Gram was my only immediate family member near me in California. I can't adequately describe how much I loved her. Ryan and I often stayed with her when we were kids, and she was so good to us. Both she and my grandfather showered us with love and great food, and gave us fun things to do. Even in recent years, I looked forward to seeing Gram every Sunday night when I drove the forty-minute route to her home for a visit. Although she had not been completely coherent for the past seven years (my uncle lived with her and was her caregiver), she always recognized me when I arrived and was happy to see me. Her eyes would brighten, and she'd announce with a smile, "Wellll . . . there's my little sweetie."

If you have a beloved grandparent, you can understand why Gram was precious to me. Her death created a tremendous void in my life. Although I'm grateful to God for giving me more years with her than I could have expected, I wasn't prepared to deal with her sudden passing. There is never a convenient time to say good-bye to someone you love.

To make matters worse, my fifteen-year-old cat became seriously ill during the same week my grandmother passed away. As I wrote in my book *Let's Talk!*, my female calico cat Kid-Wid and I had a rocky start to our relationship. Since then, we learned to love and appreciate each other, although not without an occasional standoff in moments of disagreement. For the most part, though, our relationship was tranquil. I enjoyed how she greeted me at the door and slept on my bed each night. She and I were the only occupants in my home, and that made her extra special.

So there I was several months ago, grieving the loss of Gram while preparing a slide show for her memorial service, and tending to my sick cat at the same time. When I took Kid-Wid to the veterinarian, he told me that she was most likely suffering from kidney disease, which is common and often fatal in older cats. He said I could provide treatment and medication for a couple of days and see if she experienced a turnaround.

For two nights my friend Loreen brought over a variety of cat foods, and we tried everything to encourage Kid-Wid to eat. We even opened cans of salmon and tuna meant for humans, mixed it with mayonnaise, and smeared it onto her paws in the hope that she'd lick it off. At best, Kid-Wid would only sniff at the food, lick and nibble a bit, and call it quits. Hardly a meal. I realized that I was rapidly losing my furry friend.

The day after my grandmother's memorial service, I prayed again about what to do with Kid-Wid. When I phoned the vet, his words seemed to provide the answer I was seeking when he said, "If Kid-Wid isn't eating, she can't possibly feel good. I think the most humane thing to do at this point would be to euthanize her." In other words, put her to sleep; end her life.

When I hung up the phone, I knew I had to do what was best for Kid-Wid: I had to let the doctor end her suffering.

Loreen met me at the vet's office that evening. I had a lump in my throat as I asked her to take a few photos of Kid-Wid and me in front of the bushes outside the medical building. I wanted some memories of my feline friend to treasure because I didn't have any recent pictures of the two of us. After our little photo session, I placed my sick kitty in Loreen's arms and asked her to hand her to the nurse. I also gave her Kid-Wid's favorite toy mouse to be with her when the end came.

While my caring friend was inside the vet's office, I circled around the parking lot and prayed these words under my breath: "Lord, I know we all go through hard times, but it's so painful to lose Gram and my cat in the same week." Tears pooled in my eyes as I prayed.

When Loreen emerged from the double doors, we shared a long hug. Then she said, "I'm house-sitting for a lady who owns seven cats. Would you like to get your 'cat needs' met by driving over there with me?" I smiled through my tears and said, "I think that would help." So off we went. After two hours of hanging out with the critters—playing, petting, cuddling—Loreen and I had dinner at a Mexican restaurant and then picked up some frozen yogurt. I was thankful to the Lord for providing me with my friend's company so I didn't have to be alone that night.

The next day was even more difficult, but I kept myself occupied with work-related matters. When the sun went down, however, I became very depressed. I kept going back and forth in my mind between the two losses of my grandmother and my pet—crying over one or the other. Fortunately, I had made plans that evening to drive to Palm Springs to join my parents at a resort. The Lord had once again arranged for me not to be alone. Almost immediately upon arrival, my grief began to lift. Spending time with my mom and dad, and receiving their hugs and soothing words, was just what I needed. With each passing day, the shock of losing my beloved grandmother and my furry friend lessened, and the pain became more manageable. By the end of the week, although still in grief, I was strong enough to go home.

Why did I share that story with you? I wanted you to see how the Lord cared for me in the midst of painful circumstances. Consider the ways He demonstrated His love for me during that traumatic week:

- He arranged for my parents to be within driving distance when my grandmother passed away.
- He ministered to my wounded heart through thoughtful friends who called and sent cards and e-mails, assuring me of their prayers.
- He provided His strength and comfort.
- He sent a friend to my home on two consecutive nights to help care for my sick kitty.
- He allowed me to get through my grandmother's memorial service before I had to make a decision about what to do with Kid-Wid.
- When it became necessary to have my pet put to sleep, He sent Loreen to assist me.
- After that traumatic event, the Lord arranged for me to spend time with Loreen and seven cats that needed affection.

- The following night, He once again kept me from being alone by enabling me to leave town and spend time with my parents.
- He gave me a week with my folks at a resort to lessen my pain.
- He directed me to Scriptures that provided strength and comfort in my time of need.

When I reread that list, I'm reminded of Psalm 46:1, which says, "God is our refuge and strength, an ever-present help in trouble." Although He doesn't always prevent us from going through intense suffering, He does promise to help us get through it. "I am the LORD, your God, who takes hold of your right hand and says to you, Do not fear; I will help you" (Isaiah 41:13).

In the same way that He cared for me in my time of need, He will be there for you in your difficult times. All you need to do is ask prayerfully. The Bible instructs you to "cast all your anxiety upon him because he cares for you" (1 Peter 5:7). There is no reason to be worried about *anything*, because the Lord will see you through your darkest days. "Trust in him at all times, O people; pour out your hearts to him, for God is our refuge" (Psalm 62:8).

Before I conclude this chapter, I have some good news to share: less than two weeks after Kid-Wid died, a friend e-mailed me about a two-month-old female calico kitten that needed a home. He told me that if I was interested, I could have her.

Of course I was very interested! Originally I was going to wait a few months before looking for a new cat, but it appeared the Lord had arranged for me to adopt one much sooner. All I had to do was drive to my friend's house and pick her up.

I've now had the little ball of fur for several months, and we've become good friends. I've named her Punkin, an affectionate name that goes with her autumn coloring. She likes to crawl in my lap while I'm at the computer, give nose kisses, and sleep near me on my bed. Even now while I'm writing, she is curled beside me on the sofa, resting her head on my arm.

Little Punkin has lifted my spirits by bringing joy and comfort at a difficult time. Her companionship is a gift from the Lord to me, and one more demonstration of His love.

LET'S TALK ABOUT ANXIETY

ALYSON THOMAS (student, age 16): I've found that reading Psalms and Proverbs helps to strengthen me during difficult times. Just today I read a proverb about how the Lord is a tower of refuge, and the righteous run to it and are protected. That made me feel so secure.

SAMANTHA BOWSER (student, age 17): Before I go to bed I always talk to God about whatever is on my mind. Sometimes I'll keep babbling for thirty minutes or more to get some things off my chest. I'm one of those people who can't sleep if something is wrong, so it helps to give everything to God and know that He's handling it.

REBECCA YOUNG (student, age 16): I get stressed about school. I've had a lot of friend-related problems since seventh grade, and right now I don't feel like I have anyone at school I can talk to. I do know a couple of girls—one of them used to be my best friend—but they ignore me at times, so right now I don't have one person at school I would consider a good friend. I've been praying about that and waiting to see how God is going to answer.

PAUL HONTZ *(student, age 19): Middle school was a difficult stage for me, but it was during that time of trial that I learned how to really trust God.*

ALYSON THOMAS *(student, age 16): When I'm going through a tough time, I like to sit in silence and talk to God. I ask Him to help calm me down. After I've done that for a couple of days in a row, I always feel more at peace with my circumstances.*

SARAH UTTERBACK *(student, age 16): Sometimes when I'm depressed or anxious, I'll ask God to speak to me through His Word, and then I'll open my Bible at random. Strange as it may seem, it's amazing how often my eyes will land on a verse that ties in with what I'm going through! I'll say out loud, "God, you are so here right now!" And it's interesting how a verse can impact me in a certain way, and then I'll read the same verse six months later, and it will relate to something completely different that I'm going through. That's the power of Scripture—it really is sharper than a double-edged sword.*

MARY SPAGNOLA *(student, age 16): We have to have faith that God is going to get us through whatever we're dealing with. For me, my faith is strengthened by reading the Bible daily. When I was in eighth grade, Psalm 91 helped me a lot during a painful experience. It talks about how much God loves me, cares for me, and protects me.*

DUSTY SANDERSON *(student, age 17): I'm going through a difficult time now while playing on my school's baseball* *team. I'm the only Christian on the team, so it's hard to be an example when a lot of guys are using bad language and tearing each other down in a joking way. They have a "whatever" type of attitude—just wanting to mess around and have a good time. I'm a leader on the team, so I try to boost the energy level, but everybody keeps pulling it down. I deal with that almost every day, but what has helped me is to read my Bible and concentrate on what God says about being faithful and about being a light when surrounded by darkness.*

MATT GODSHALL *(student, age 14): The day before Christmas Eve my dad was diagnosed with brain cancer. There's no cure for the type of cancer he has, and the average life expectancy is about a year. It's been really tough for everyone in my family, but in some ways it's brought us together. Before my dad was diagnosed, he and his dad didn't get along and didn't care about each other. But since my dad's diagnosis, my grandfather has flown from another state to visit him, and their relationship has improved—in fact, it's better than it's ever been. I can see the Lord working to bring something good out of something bad.*

PASTOR LUKE CUNNINGHAM *(youth minister): When David went up against Goliath, he wasn't thinking,* Can I defeat Goliath? *He was thinking,* God will defeat Goliath! *Then David picked up a stone and crushed the giant's skull. We tend to measure our problems against ourselves, and when we do that we can't conquer them. God is always going to be bigger than our problems! We just need to turn them over to Him and trust that He's going to win the battle.* ❀

What Say You?

1) Describe a time when God helped you through a painful circumstance.

2) Do you believe that the Lord will be there for you in every situation?

3) How does God want you to respond when difficult times come?

Your Glorious Heritage

Check it out:

Romans 8:17

Here's a lighthearted fact about me you may not have guessed: I like Disney princesses. Okay, so you're either thinking, *That's great—so do I*, or *Gimme a break!* Regardless, I've always enjoyed the fantasy aspect of Cinderella, Snow White, Belle, and Sleeping Beauty. These animated heroines brought me a lot of joy throughout my childhood and beyond.

Although this "princess interest" isn't something I've devoted much time or thought to, I really love the films and occasionally buy something from the never-ending array of movie-themed merchandise. Recently I bought a Cinderella carriage purse at Disneyland that I'm using to hold hair clips. While I was making the purchase, the salesgirl asked, "Is this for your daughter?" I smiled and said, "No, it's for me." I could tell by her expression she was thinking, *Okaaaaay*. She probably thought I was going to swing the purse as I walked down Park Avenue in a fancy dress and stilettos. Whatever. I'm not ashamed of liking Disney princesses. I've even been known to give my girlfriends Sleeping Beauty birthday cards and wrap their gifts in Cinderella paper.

A couple of years ago, I was browsing a Disney gift shop with my friend Lauren. As we passed the Snow White dolls, Lauren surprised me when she said rather cynically, "I think the princess ideology damaged us when we were kids—you know, the whole concept of fairy tales, true love, and dreams coming true. It created unrealistic expectations." I had to admit she had a good point, but I found her statement a little depressing. Could it have been motivated by the fact she had yet to find Prince Charming?

I haven't found my knight in shining armor either, but I've never taken fairy tales seriously enough to develop a chip on my shoulder. I've always known real life isn't about wishing upon a star and living happily ever after. Besides, I tried wishing on a star a long time ago, and it didn't work!

Occasionally I see little girls twirling in their Disney princess costumes. I know they expect their life to be charmed, just like the characters they're impersonating. I wish they could live in a protective kingdom that would allow them to feel like royalty and see their dreams come true, but life holds no guarantees. It would be awesome if everyone saw their hopes fulfilled, but our corrupt world is not the Magic Kingdom. At the risk of sounding like my disillusioned friend Lauren, let me say that each of us runs the risk of being wounded, rejected, and even dumped. It reminds me of the song "Here in the Real World" by country artist Alan Jackson. In one verse, he mentions how life would be so sweet if it were like the movies. But as he sings in the chorus:

> *The boy don't always get the girl*
> *Here in the real world.*

And the girl don't always get the boy, either. Even if you win your Prince Charming, there will be days when he'll cause you to feel like less than a princess. Yes, there is such a thing as living happily ever after, but not in this lifetime.

Now, before you trash your imaginary crown, may I suggest you polish it to a shimmering glow and place it back on your head. There is Someone who will *always* treat you like a precious princess—your Lord and Savior, Jesus Christ! If you've received Him into your heart, the Bible says you're a child of the King of kings and you've been promised a distinguished place in His eternal Kingdom (see Colossians 1:12). That means you're royalty! And how much does Jesus love you? Enough to go to the cross and die for your sins to purchase a place in heaven for you. Now *that* is genuine love!

Since Jesus values you to such an extent, there's no reason to hang your head and feel like a loser, regardless of what anyone says or does. Remember whom you belong to—the King of kings! That means you're very special.

Take a moment to read the following list, which describes how valuable you are to the Lord.

My Identity in Christ

Romans 8:1	There is no condemnation for me, because I'm in Christ Jesus.
Colossians 1:13	I have been brought into His Kingdom, delivered from the power of darkness.
1 John 3:1	I am God's child.
Galatians 4:6-7	All that God has is mine.

Ephesians 1:5	I have been adopted by God.
Ephesians 2:19	I am part of His family.
Hebrews 4:16	I have access to God at any moment.
Romans 3:24	I am justified—my sins have been forgiven through Christ.
Romans 8:17	I am one of God's heirs, and I'm a joint heir with Christ.
1 Timothy 6:17	God provides for me.
John 15:15	I am a friend of Christ.
1 Corinthians 12:13	I have been baptized into Christ's body.
Nahum 1:7	God protects and cares for me.
1 Corinthians 3:16	My body is Christ's temple—a vessel in which His Spirit dwells.
John 15:5	I am a branch in the Vine (Christ).
Colossians 1:14	I have received the free gift of forgiveness.
1 Thessalonians 4:8	I have received the free gift of the Holy Spirit.
1 John 5:11	I have received the free gift of eternal life.
Psalm 138:8	I have purpose and destiny while I'm here on earth.
Ephesians 1:14	I am God's special possession.

1 Peter 5:8-10	I am able to resist the devil.
1 Thessalonians 1:4	I am chosen by God and dearly loved by Him.
Ephesians 1:1	I am a saint.
Ephesians 2:10	I am created to do good works that God has planned for me.
Revelation 21:9	I am the bride of Christ.
Colossians 3:4	I have life in Christ.
2 Corinthians 5:17	I am a new creation.
1 Corinthians 6:17	I am joined to the Lord, and I'm one in spirit with Him.
Matthew 5:14	I am the light of the world.
Matthew 5:13	I am the salt of the earth.
Psalm 61:5	I have a glorious heritage.
1 John 5:11	I am eternal.
1 Corinthians 9:25	I will receive a crown that lasts forever.
Colossians 3:4	I will appear with Christ in glory!

Isn't that a beautiful description of your spiritual heritage? On the days when you feel insignificant, take time to reread this list and think about how important you are to Jesus. Ask Him to help you perceive yourself the way He views you: as someone who has been given a position of honor and dignity—the daughter of the King!

Kind of shatters the concept of the glass slipper, doesn't it?

LET'S TALK ABOUT SELF-WORTH

SAMANTHA BOWSER (student, age 17): My family members are intelligent, and I've never felt like I was the brightest one in the bunch. I've often thought there was something wrong with me. But I know that God has a plan for my life, and even though I'm not a genius, I'm going to end up doing exactly what He intended for me to do. Being aware of that has given me peace, even though I may never get high educational degrees.

MARY SPAGNOLA (student, age 16): I've read in Job 38 about how God laid the foundation of the earth, and I've read in other places in the Bible that He wants to have a relationship with me. When I meditate on those two things, it really builds my self-confidence!

SARAH UTTERBACK (student, age 16): Prayer is my number one outlet. Whenever I feel like I'm not pretty enough or I don't have enough friends (or the right friends) or I don't have the most understanding parents in the world, I take it to the Lord in prayer. It's such a comfort to know that in the lowest of times, I can give my burdens to God and He'll carry them.

MRS. FRANCES LEAF (high school psychologist): One of the most important things I'd like teens to realize is that high school is not the end of their lives. For a lot of students, grades nine through twelve are difficult. My daughter hated her high school experience, but she's now a college freshman and is having the time of her life! She's noticed that people in college seem to be more accepting of those who are different or who have various interests. For example, my daughter is into art and art history, and nobody discriminates against her for that. She feels freedom to be herself.

MR. TIMOTHY STRANSKE *(high school teacher): A lot of teens worry that their peers aren't going to accept them. I want to encourage girls to persevere, because life will improve in that way once they get out of middle school and high school. As people grow older, they don't scrutinize others to such an extent.*

MR. MATT NORTHRUP *(high school dean): This is what I'd like girls to comprehend: in Psalm 139:14, you are described as being "fearfully and wonderfully made." Let those words truly sink in as you meditate upon them. You are precious, beautiful, unique, and extraordinary. You are cared for, and you are loved. There is nothing you can do to be loved more by God. There isn't a certain body type you need to have, a specific grade point average you need to acquire, or a particular college you must attend. Please know that you are beautiful and extraordinarily important, not because of what you have accomplished, but because of the value the Lord has placed upon your life.* ✿

What Say You?

1) Do you have days when you feel insignificant? If so, what can you do to increase your confidence?

2) How do you know that you're considered royalty by God (see Colossians 1:12)?

3) What was the ultimate sacrifice that Jesus made to demonstrate His love for you?

4) Name three blessings you have been given through your relationship with Christ.

Eternally Yours

A good defining Scripture for this book is 1 Thessalonians 5:11, which says, "Encourage one another and build each other up, just as in fact you are doing."

In keeping with that biblical concept, I hope you have found the preceding discussions helpful as we've talked about everything from dating issues to developing a healthy self-image.

More important, I hope you have seen how the Bible is the greatest resource for every area of your life, providing insight, direction, and God's eternal promises. You can embrace the Bible as absolute truth and trust in it completely. Everything else in this world will pass away, but the Word of God will stand firm throughout eternity: "The grass withers and the flowers fall, but the word of our God stands forever" (Isaiah 40:8).

Speaking of that which is eternal, I'd like to ask you a very significant question: Can you remember a time when you trusted in Jesus as your Savior by inviting Him into your heart and life? I can vividly recall my own experience at the age of five. My dad and I were sitting on the bed, having a chat. It was a Sunday night. Dad was wearing a white T-shirt. He explained the gospel message and asked if I'd like to receive Jesus. I agreed without hesitation, and we prayed a simple prayer together (sometimes called "the sinner's prayer"). Even though I was very young with a limited knowledge of God, I understood that I was a sinner in need of His forgiveness. That's the beauty of the gospel message—even a child can comprehend it.

Since that time, I've often reflected back to that life-changing decision I made as a five-year-old kid. Through years of trials and triumphs, I've always known that I belong to the Lord and am part of His eternal Kingdom.

Many people believe they don't need to receive Christ to be worthy of going to heaven. They think that because they've tried to be "good" and have never done anything horrific, like murdering someone or robbing a bank, they are acceptable to God. Not true. The Bible makes it clear that none of us are qualified for heaven on our own: "All have sinned and fall short of the glory of God" (Romans 3:23). Even if we only sinned one time in our entire lives, we would still be unworthy, because God expects us to be absolutely perfect: "Be perfect, therefore, as your heavenly Father is perfect" (Matthew 5:48).

Our sin and God's demand for perfection create a major problem! But here's the wonderful news: God solved that problem by sending His sinless, perfect Son, Jesus Christ, to this earth to die for our sins and purchase a place in heaven for us. Because of that great act of love, we can know for certain that we have eternal life. "I write these things to you who believe in the name of the Son of God so that you may know that you have eternal life" (1 John 5:13).

If you have never accepted that free gift of mercy, the offer is still open. All you need to do is acknowledge that Jesus is the Son of God who died and was raised from the dead, ask Him to forgive your sins, and invite Him to be Lord of your life (Romans 10:9-10). It's that simple. The result is that you will become a new creation in Christ (see 2 Corinthians 5:17)!

Giving your heart to the Lord is the single most important decision you will ever make, and you will never regret it. For me personally, the privilege of knowing Jesus and discovering His immeasurable love for me has brought meaning to my life in a way I could never experience through worldly gain. I have a sense of belonging, and I know where I am going when I leave this planet someday. That's the hope that has been given to me through Christ!

If you would like to experience the same riches in your own personal relationship with Jesus, I invite you to talk to the Lord right now. Pray something like this: "Lord, I am so sorry for the wickedness in my life and the times I have disappointed You. I believe that You died for my sins and rose from the dead to give me eternal life. Thank You for taking the punishment I deserve. Please forgive me and come to live within me right now. I will do my best to serve You faithfully and tell others about what You have done for me. I now belong to You forever. Amen."

If you sincerely prayed to be saved, congratulations! You are now a member of the family of God. The Bible says that the angels in heaven are rejoicing because of your decision (see Luke 15:10). Imagine that!

May I urge you to get involved in a Christian Bible study with a leader who understands Scripture and can help you apply it to your life? (A local church youth group might be a possibility.) I'd also like to encourage you to begin talking to the Lord each day in prayer and reading His Word. The book of John in the New Testament is a good place to start.

With that, we have now come to a good place to end. As always, I would love to hear from you if you would like to write. You can reach me at Focus on the Family, Colorado Springs, Colorado 80920.

May God bless you, and keep pressing on!

Forgetting what is behind and straining toward what is ahead, I press on toward the goal to win the prize for which God has called me heavenward in Christ Jesus.
PHILIPPIANS 3:13-14

About the Author

Let's Walk the Talk! is Danae Dobson's second nonfiction project. This inspirational book is a sequel to her former publication for adolescent girls entitled *Let's Talk!* Danae is also active in her speaking ministry, addressing women at church-related events such as banquets, teas, and conferences. She is also involved in seminars for teens and speaks to children at Christian schools.

Danae was born in Southern California and wrote her first children's manuscript, *Woof! A Bedtime Story about a Dog*, at the age of twelve. Upon publication, she became the youngest author in the twenty-five-year history of that publishing house. It's a title that she still holds today.

In 1990 she received her bachelor's degree in communication from Azusa Pacific University. She has authored twenty-three books to date, including the popular Woof series that was spun off of her original story. These best-selling books have sold more than 400,000 copies and have also been released in the United Kingdom and Indonesia. Other works include *Parables for Kids* (coauthored with Dr. James Dobson), the Forest Friends series, and the Sunny Street Kids' Club series. Danae has appeared on *The 700 Club* and *Time for Hope*, and she has been a guest on more than one hundred radio broadcasts, including *Minirth Meier* and *Focus on the Family*. She has also been a featured speaker at the Christian Booksellers Association, Hawaiian Islands Ministries, MOPS, and numerous Christian schools.

Danae is the daughter of Dr. James and Shirley Dobson of Focus on the Family ministry, and has a younger brother, Ryan, who is also an author, a speaker, and an Internet radio host. Danae resides in Southern California.

let's talk!

Good stuff for girlfriends about God, guys, and growing up

Danae Dobson

If you're looking for some more friendly

conversation and big-sister advice . . .

check out *Let's Talk!*, also by Danae Dobson.